Teatime
BIRTHDAYS

Teatime
BIRTHDAYS

*Afternoon-Tea Celebrations
for All Ages*

83PRESS

Hoffman Media
1900 International Park Drive, Suite 50
Birmingham, Alabama 35243
hoffmanmedia.com

ISBN # 978-1-940772-76-9
Printed in China

ON THE COVER:
(Front Cover) Desserts from
"Sweet Celebration," pages 97–98.
(Back Cover) Lemon-Ginger Cake, page 25

Contents

Introduction

BIRTHDAYS PROVIDE, PERHAPS, THE BEST REASON OF ALL TO CELEBRATE. Whether you throw a tea party for your own birthday in order to treat your dearest friends, or whether you honor a loved one on their special day, there's just something uniquely memorable about celebrating the annual milestone with afternoon tea. Some might argue that it's the warm scones or the delicious sandwiches and other petite savories or maybe the decadent desserts, all served with bountiful pots of hot tea, that make teatime an enjoyable experience. But more than likely, most will say that what they treasure most is time to connect with those they hold dear, and that the tasty fare and tea served at a festively adorned table truly are the proverbial icing on the cake.

Teatime Birthdays showcases 10 celebrations, each with its own unique aesthetic. From elegant to modern to whimsical, there is something for all ages and genders. Girls and ladies will swoon at the dainty, feminine offerings, but boys and gentlemen will also find several menus and table settings designed with them in mind. And naturally, each includes a cake. Some of the cakes are large, while others take the form of cupcakes or other personal-size treats. All are, however, delicious and perfect for the occasion.

To give you ease in entertaining, there are tips for hosting a crowd (page 10), and our "Tea-Steeping Guide" (page 14) gives guidelines for preparing the perfect pot of tea. The tea pairings for every menu have been expertly curated to assure the infusion you serve complements the fare and theme. Whenever possible, recipes include make-ahead tips for food preparation so you can focus on other priorities the day of the party. And if you're concerned about entertaining guests who have gluten sensitivities, you will find the index on page 135 to be of great help, as it highlights recipes that are completely gluten-free.

We think you and your guests will agree that having a tea party is one of the best ways to wish someone, "Happy Birthday!"

Hosting Tea
FOR A CROWD

Birthday celebrations can be intimate gatherings, but other times, they might call for a guest list larger than that for a typical tea party. When faced with the task of preparing tea for a group, these helpful tips will ensure your event is a success whether you're a novice or an expert tea-party host.

EXTENDING INVITATIONS

Formal invitations are a lovely and thoughtful way to communicate the details of the upcoming event, as well as to be sure you have an accurate count of those who will attend. Although invitations printed or written by hand and mailed are certainly preferred, technology has made it acceptable to extend them via telephone or e-mail. However you choose to spread the word of your teatime celebration, plan early. Ideally, invitees should receive the communication a minimum of two weeks before the party. Invitations should include the following information:

- *Date and time of the event* (between 2:00 and 5:00 p.m., with 4:00 p.m. being preferred for afternoon tea. If the format is a come-and-go reception, give a time range, such as 2:00 to 4:00 p.m.)

- *Address of venue*

- *Name of honoree(s)*

- *Name of host(s)*

- *Information and deadline for RSVP*

- *Preferred attire* (Specify only if clothing should be more formal or more casual than usual for afternoon tea or if costumes are encouraged.)

- *Gifts* (Specify only if gifts are not preferred or if they are to be given to a special cause, such as a charity.)

SELECTING AND SERVING HOT TEA

When choosing the types of tea to serve, offer a choice of at least two to accompany and complement your food selections. (The menus in this book feature a tea pairing for each of the courses.) Generally, strongly scented teas should be avoided unless they are favorites of the honoree. Instead, opt for classic blends, single-origin teas, or favorite fruit-flavored infusions. Having a caffeine-free alternative is a thoughtful gesture children and other caffeine-sensitive guests will appreciate.

• *Use loose-leaf tea rather than prebagged. (See our "Tea-Steeping Guide" on page 14 for more information.)*

• *Make tea an hour or two ahead, and keep it hot in insulated urns or thermal carafes in the kitchen until ready to serve. (Do not use containers that have ever held coffee, as the lingering oils from the coffee will impart an unpleasant taste to the tea.)*

• *In the kitchen, warm teapots with hot water, discard water, and fill teapots with hot tea from urns or carafes just before serving. (Let tea cool before serving it to children.)*

• *During the party, filled teapots can be placed on tea warmers (stands outfitted with tea lights) on the serving table or on individual tables, if desired. Because it is not possible to regulate the heat they produce, resulting in scorched tea, tea warmers are not suitable for keeping tea hot for long periods. (To prevent burns, please make sure children are closely supervised.) Tea cozies are a safe alternative to tea warmers and are available in many pretty and practical designs.*

• *Select several friends to ensure that pots and cups remain full throughout the event. Having others assist with this task allows you ample time to give guests your full attention while remaining a dutiful host, especially during a buffet-style tea party. So your pourers can still enjoy the tea party, write down a set schedule in which each person serves for no longer than 20 minutes.*

PREPARING THE FOOD

Tea fare is usually best when made just before serving. Unless you have a lot of help in the kitchen, it is often logistically impossible to wait until the day of the event to prepare the food. Many of the recipes in this book include a "MAKE-AHEAD TIP" section, but general tips for making favorite teatime fare in advance follow.

- *Scones*—Freeze raw scones on parchment-lined baking sheets. Once frozen, transfer scones to airtight containers or bags, and store in the freezer for up to a month. Just before serving, place desired quantity of frozen scones (do not thaw) on parchment-lined baking sheets, and bake in a preheated oven according to recipe, allowing an additional 5 to 10 minutes for adequate doneness and browning, if necessary.
- *Tea Sandwiches*—Most fillings can be made a day ahead and stored in the refrigerator. Assemble sandwiches a few hours before the tea party, drape with damp paper towels, cover well with plastic wrap, and refrigerate until needed.
- *Sweets*—Most cakes and cookies can be made at least a week in advance. Wrap cake layers tightly with plastic wrap, and place cookies in airtight containers with layers separated by wax paper. Store in the freezer for up to a week. Thaw completely before frosting or filling.

SETTING UP A BUFFET-STYLE TEA

The way you set up the food and tea can help avoid congestion when serving buffet style. If possible, arrange the plates, napkins, pastry forks, small knives, and food on one table, and place the teapots, cups and saucers, teaspoons, and any condiments for the hot tea (milk, sugar and/or honey, and lemon slices) on a sideboard or a wet bar. If beverages and food will be served from the same table, group the tea things on the right end of the surface so guests can serve themselves tea fare first and pick up the hot tea last.

- *Snack plates—dishes with allotted space for a teacup—are a good alternative to traditional plates, cups, and saucers if partygoers will be standing while eating and drinking tea.*
- *When preparing food, planning for 2 or 3 of each item per guest can help prevent empty platters early into the party.*
- *Clearly designate a small table or other surface for used dishes.*

TEA-STEEPING *Guide*

The quality of the tea served at afternoon tea is as important as the food and the décor. To be sure your infusion is successful every time, here are some basic guidelines to follow.

WATER

Always use the best water possible. If the water tastes good, so will your tea. Heat the water on the stove top or in an electric kettle to the desired temperature. A microwave oven is not recommended.

TEMPERATURE

Heating the water to the correct temperature is arguably one of the most important factors in making a great pot of tea. Pouring boiling water on green, white, or oolong tea leaves can result in a very unpleasant brew. Always refer to the tea purveyor's packaging for specific instructions, but in general, use 170° to 195° water for these delicate tea types. Reserve boiling (212°) water for black and puerh teas, as well as herbal and fruit tisanes.

TEAPOT

If the teapot you plan to use is delicate, warm it with hot tap water first to avert possible cracking. Discard this water before adding the tea leaves or tea bags.

TEA

Use the highest-quality tea you can afford, whether loose leaf or prepackaged in bags or sachets. Remember that these better teas can often be steeped more than once. When using loose-leaf tea, generally use 1 generous teaspoon of dry leaf per 8 ounces of water, and use an infuser basket. For a stronger infusion, add another teaspoonful or two of dry tea leaf.

TIME

As soon as the water reaches the correct temperature for the type of tea, pour it over the leaves or tea bag in the teapot, and cover the pot with a lid. Set a timer—usually 1 to 2 minutes for whites and oolongs; 2 to 3 minutes for greens; and 3 to 5 minutes for blacks, puerhs, and herbals. (Steeping tea longer than recommended can yield a bitter infusion.) When the timer goes off, remove the infuser basket or the tea bags from the teapot.

ENJOYMENT

For best flavor, serve the tea as soon as possible. Keep the beverage warm atop a lighted warmer or under your favorite tea cozy if necessary.

A STYLISH

Celebration

The
MENU

SCONE
Brie, Pear & Thyme Scones
Blue Moon Tea

SAVORIES
Caprese Chicken Canapés
Asian Avocado-Salmon Canapés
Zucchini Rolls
with Mini Mushrooms
Korea Green Jeoncha Organic

SWEETS
Pistachio-Topped Chocolate
Shortbread Cookies
Blackberry-Rosemary
Custard Ice Cream
Lemon-Ginger Cake
*Organic Sweet Colombian Black Tea
(Wiry 2)*

Tea Pairings by Simpson & Vail
800-282-8327 • svtea.com

*A table with rich hues,
a contemporary motif,
and uniquely designed
fare are picturesque for
a trendsetter's birthday
tea party.*

Brie, Pear & Thyme Scones

Makes 14

½ cup finely diced (¼-inch) peeled pears
   (Anjou or Bosc)
1 teaspoon fresh lemon juice
3 cups all-purpose flour
2 tablespoons granulated sugar
2 tablespoons fresh thyme leaves
4 teaspoons baking powder
½ teaspoon salt
½ cup cold unsalted butter, cubed
⅔ cup cubed (¼-inch) Brie cheese
1¼ cups cold heavy whipping cream, divided

• Preheat oven to 375°. Line a rimmed baking sheet with parchment paper.
• In a medium bowl, toss pear in lemon juice until coated. Place pears on paper towels, and let drain.
• In a large bowl, whisk together flour, sugar, thyme, baking powder, and salt. Using a pastry blender or 2 forks, cut cold butter into flour mixture until it resembles coarse crumbs. Add cheese, stirring until well combined. (If there are any large pieces of cheese, use pastry blender or forks to break them up). Add 1 cup plus 2 tablespoons cold cream to flour mixture, stirring until a dough begins to form. (If dough seems dry and dough won't come together, add more cream, 1 tablespoon at a time.) Working gently, bring mixture together with hands until a dough forms.
• Turn out dough onto a lightly floured surface, and knead gently until smooth by patting dough and folding it in half 4 to 5 times. Using a rolling pin, roll out dough to a 12x9-inch rectangle. Scatter pears over half of dough. Fold other half of dough over pears to enclose them. Lightly roll out dough again to a ¾-inch thickness. Using a 2¼-inch round cutter dipped in flour, cut 14 scones from dough without twisting cutter, rerolling scraps only once. Place scones 2 inches apart on prepared baking sheet.
• Brush tops of scones with remaining 2 tablespoons cream.
• Bake until scones are golden brown, 18 to 22 minutes. Let cool on baking sheet for 5 minutes. Serve warm or at room temperature.

RECOMMENDED CONDIMENT:
Orange Marmalade

Caprese Chicken Canapés

Makes 8

2 tablespoons white balsamic vinegar
1 tablespoon olive oil
1½ teaspoons mayonnaise
⅛ teaspoon kosher salt
1 cup finely diced rotisserie chicken
2 tablespoons chopped fresh basil
4 slices pumpernickel bread, toasted
4 slices fresh mozzarella cheese*
24 small tomato halves*
Garnish: fresh basil leaves

• In a medium bowl, whisk together vinegar, olive oil, mayonnaise, and salt. Add chicken and chopped basil, stirring until combined.
• Using a 1½-inch round cutter, cut 8 rounds from bread slices and 4 rounds from cheese slices. Using a knife, cut cheese rounds in half horizontally to make 8 thin rounds.
• In the same cutter placed on a flat surface or serving platter, layer 1 bread round, 1 cheese round, and 1½ table-spoons chicken salad. Using fingers, gently press chicken salad to compact. Carefully remove cutter from canapé. Repeat with remaining bread, cheese, and chicken salad. Top each canapé with 3 tomato halves. Serve immedi-ately, or cover and refrigerate for up to 1 hour.
• Garnish with basil leaves, if desired.

We used BelGioioso presliced cheese and Sprinkles tomatoes.

MAKE-AHEAD TIP: *Chicken salad and cheese rounds can be prepared separately a day ahead, covered, and refrigerated until needed.*

Asian Avocado-Salmon Canapés

Makes 8

2 medium avocados, mashed
1 teaspoon tamari sauce
1 teaspoon fresh lemon juice
½ teaspoon grated fresh ginger
4 slices marbled rye bread, toasted
2 (4-ounce) packages thinly sliced smoked salmon
Garnish: sesame seeds

• In a small bowl, stir together avocados, tamari sauce, lemon juice, and ginger until combined.
• Using a 1½-inch square cutter, cut 8 squares from

bread slices and 16 squares from salmon slices.
• In the same cutter placed on a flat surface or serving platter, layer 1 bread square, 1½ teaspoons avocado mixture, and 2 salmon squares. Using fingers, gently press salmon down to compact avocado mixture. Carefully remove cutter from canapé. Repeat with remaining bread, avocado mixture, and salmon. Serve immediately, or cover and refrigerate for up to 1 hour.
• Garnish with sesame seeds, if desired.

Zucchini Rolls with Mini Mushrooms

Makes 16

16 zucchini ribbons*
¼ teaspoon kosher salt
1 (100-gram) package bunashimeji mushrooms, divided
1 tablespoon olive oil
1 (8-ounce) package cream cheese
1 tablespoon fresh lemon juice
2 tablespoons chopped fresh tarragon leaves
Garnish: fresh tarragon sprigs

• Line a rimmed baking sheet with paper towels.
• Place zucchini ribbons on prepared baking sheet. Sprinkle zucchini with salt. Refrigerate, uncovered, for 1 hour.
• Reserve 32 to 48 mushrooms for garnish. Chop remaining mushrooms.
• In a small saucepan, combine oil and chopped mush-rooms; cook over medium-high heat until mushrooms are tender and moisture is cooked out, 5 to 7 minutes. Reduce heat to low. Add cream cheese and lemon juice, stirring until combined. Transfer mushroom mixture to a separate bowl. Let cool to room temperature. Fold in chopped tarragon. Cover and refrigerate until chilled, approximately 30 minutes.
• Pat zucchini ribbons dry with paper towels. Place approximately 1½ teaspoons mushroom mixture 1 inch from a short end of each ribbon. Beginning at that short end, roll zucchini ribbon over mushroom mixture, taking care not to push filling out sides. Stand zucchini rolls on fresh paper towels. Place several reserved mushrooms in opening at top of roll, covering the filling. Refrigerate until ready to serve.
• Garnish with tarragon leaves, if desired. Serve immediately.

To make zucchini ribbons using a mandoline, cut ¹⁄₁₆-inch-thick, lengthwise slices from 2 medium zucchinis, or drag a Y-shaped vegetable peeler the length of 2 or 3 medium zucchinis.

Pistachio-Topped Chocolate Shortbread Cookies

Makes approximately 28

¾ cup unsalted butter, softened
½ cup confectioners' sugar
1 teaspoon vanilla extract
½ teaspoon salt
1¼ cup all-purpose flour
½ cup Dutch-process cocoa powder
1 (10-ounce) package chocolate melting wafers, melted according to package instructions
3 tablespoons finely chopped raw pistachios

• In a large bowl, beat butter with a mixer at medium-low speed until smooth. Add confectioners' sugar, vanilla extract, and salt, beating at medium speed until thick and creamy, approximately 2 minutes.
• In a small bowl, whisk together flour and cocoa powder. Add flour mixture to butter mixture in two additions, beating until just combined after each addition, scraping bowl as needed. Shape dough into a disk, and wrap in plastic wrap. Refrigerate until firm, approximately 1 hour.
• Preheat oven to 325°. Line several rimmed baking sheets with parchment paper.
• Using a rolling pin, roll out dough between 2 large pieces of parchment paper to a ¼-inch thickness. Freeze until firm, approximately 10 minutes. Remove top parchment sheet. Using a 1¾-inch fluted round cutter, cut cookies, rerolling scraps as necessary. (Once dough is rerolled, freeze dough before cutting more cookies.) Place cookies 1 inch apart on prepared baking sheets.
• Bake for 12 minutes. Let cool on pans for 10 minutes. Transfer cookies to wire racks, and let cool completely.
• Dip cookies in melted chocolate just past halfway point on each cookie. Immediately sprinkle pistachios in a line at top edge of chocolate. Place cookies on parchment paper, and let stand until chocolate has set.

MAKE-AHEAD TIP: Undecorated cookies can be placed in an airtight container with layers separated by wax paper and frozen for up to a month. Thaw before decorating. Store decorated cookies at room temperature in an airtight container with layers separated by wax paper for up to 3 days.

Blackberry-Rosemary Custard Ice Cream

Makes 1 quart

1 cup whole milk
1 cup heavy whipping cream
¾ cup granulated sugar, divided
⅛ teaspoon salt
1 (5-inch) sprig fresh rosemary
5 large egg yolks
1½ cups blackberries (fresh or frozen)
2 teaspoons fresh lemon juice
Garnish: fresh blackberries and fresh rosemary sprigs

• In a medium saucepan, stir together milk, cream, ½ cup sugar, and salt. Add rosemary sprig. Cook over medium heat until steaming. Turn off heat, and let rosemary steep for 10 minutes. Remove and discard rosemary.
• In a medium bowl, whisk together egg yolks and remaining ¼ cup sugar. Gradually add warm milk mixture to yolk mixture, whisking constantly. Return mixture to saucepan, and return pan to medium heat, cooking until mixture thickens and coats the back of a spoon (175° to 182° on a candy thermometer). Remove from heat. Strain custard through a fine-mesh sieve into a large bowl. Refrigerate until cold (or to chill faster, place in ice bath, stirring occasionally).
• In the container of a blender, purée blackberries, approximately 1 minute. Strain blackberries through a fine-mesh sieve into a medium bowl. Add lemon juice, stirring until combined. Cover and refrigerate until ready to spin ice cream.
• Add blackberry purée to custard, stirring until well combined. Freeze mixture in an ice cream maker according to manufacturer's instructions. Transfer to an airtight container, and freeze until firm, approximately 4 hours. Store, covered, in freezer.
• Garnish individual servings with blackberries and rosemary, if desired.

Lemon-Ginger Cake

Makes 1 (8-inch) cake, approximately 12 servings

1 cup unsalted butter, softened
2 cups granulated sugar
4 large eggs
1 tablespoon fresh lemon zest
2 tablespoons fresh lemon juice
3¼ cups cake flour
1 tablespoon baking powder
¼ teaspoon salt
1 cup whole milk
Ginger Simple Syrup (recipe follows)
Swiss Buttercream (recipe follows)
1 cup prepared lemon curd
Garnish: lemon slices, fresh blackberries,
   and minced crystallized ginger

• Preheat oven to 350°. Spray 2 (8-inch) round cake pans with baking spray with flour. Line bottoms with parchment paper.

• In a large bowl, beat together butter and sugar with a mixer at medium speed until light and fluffy, 3 to 4 minutes. Add eggs, one at a time, beating well after each addition. Add lemon zest and juice, beating until incorporated.

• In a medium bowl, whisk together flour, baking powder, and salt. Gradually add flour mixture to butter mixture alternately with milk, beginning and ending with flour mixture, beating just until combined after each addition. Divide batter between prepared pans, smoothing tops if necessary.

• Bake until a wooden pick inserted in centers comes out clean, 30 to 35 minutes. Let cool in pans for 10 minutes. Transfer cakes to wire racks, and let cool completely.

• Using a serrated knife in a gentle sawing motion, trim each cake level. Cut cakes in half horizontally to create 4 cake layers. Place a cake layer on a cake stand. Brush with Ginger Simple Syrup.

• Place ½ cup Swiss Buttercream in a piping bag with a ½-inch opening cut at the tip. Pipe a border of buttercream along outer edge of cake layer. Spoon ½ cup lemon curd inside buttercream border. Using an offset spatula, smooth curd to align with buttercream border. Top with another cake layer, and brush with Ginger Simple Syrup. Using an offset spatula, spread ¾ cup Swiss Buttercream on cake layer. Top with third cake layer, and brush with Ginger Simple Syrup. Pipe a buttercream border as before, returning any unused buttercream to bowl, and fill border with remaining ½ cup lemon curd. Top with remaining cake layer, and brush with remaining simple syrup. Reserve ½ cup Swiss Buttercream to decorate top of cake. Using an offset spatula, spread remaining buttercream on top and sides of cake. Place reserved ½ cup buttercream in a piping bag fitted with a medium open-star tip (Wilton #32). Pipe rosettes of various sizes on edge of half of top of cake.

• Garnish with lemon slices, blackberries, and crystallized ginger, if desided. Serve immediately, or refrigerate until ready to serve. Let buttercream come to room temperature before serving.

Ginger Simple Syrup

Makes approximately ⅔ cup

½ cup water
½ cup granulated sugar
1 (1½-inch) piece ginger root, peeled and cut in half

• In a small saucepan, cook water, sugar, and ginger together over medium-high heat until mixture comes to a boil and sugar dissolves. Remove from heat and pour simple syrup into a heatproof glass container. Let cool to room temperature. Remove ginger pieces, cover, and refrigerate until ready to use, up to a week.

Swiss Buttercream

Makes 5 cups

¾ cup large egg whites* (approximately 6 large eggs),
    room temperature
1¾ cups granulated sugar
2 cups unsalted butter, softened
½ teaspoon clear vanilla extract
⅛ teaspoon salt

• In the bowl of a stand mixer, whisk together egg whites and sugar by hand. Place mixer bowl over a saucepan of simmering water. Cook, whisking occasionally, until mixture registers 120° to 130° on an instant-read thermometer.
• Carefully return bowl to stand mixer. Using the whisk attachment, beat at high speed until stiff peaks form and bowl is cool to the touch, 7 to 8 minutes. Add butter, 2 tablespoons at a time, beating until combined. (If buttercream breaks, beat 2 to 3 minutes more, and the emulsion will come back together.) Add vanilla extract and salt, beating until incorporated. Use immediately, or transfer to an airtight container and refrigerate for up to 3 days. If refrigerating, let buttercream come to room temperature, and whip before using.

If desired, use pasteurized egg whites.

PARISIAN
Soirée

The MENU

SCONE
Raspberry, White Chocolate
& Lavender Scones with
Sweetened Whipped Cream
Flavors of France Signature Tea

SAVORIES
Radish Flower Canapés
Shrimp Salad Finger Sandwiches
Herbed Asparagus Quiches
Parisian Tango Signature Tea

SWEETS
Chocolate-Mascarpone Êclairs
Strawberries and Cream Macarons
Almond–Crème Fraîche Cupcakes
Fruits of Summer Signature Tea

Tea Pairings by Paris In A Cup
714-538-9411 • parisinacup.com

Teacups full of macarons are apropos party favors for guests to find awaiting at a table bedecked in pink and gold for a French-themed fête d'anniversaire.

Raspberry, White Chocolate & Lavender Scones

Makes 15

2½ cups all-purpose flour
⅓ cup plus 2 teaspoons granulated sugar, divided
3 teaspoons baking powder
½ teaspoon fine sea salt
4 tablespoons cold unsalted butter, cubed
3 ounces white chocolate, chopped
1 teaspoon dried culinary lavender
½ cup plus 2 tablespoons cold heavy whipping cream
1 large egg
½ teaspoon vanilla extract
½ cup chopped firm fresh raspberries
Sweetened Whipped Cream (recipe follows)
Garnish: 15 fresh raspberries

- Preheat oven to 350°. Line a rimmed baking sheet with parchment paper.
- In a large bowl, whisk together flour, ⅓ cup sugar, baking powder, and salt. Using a pastry blender or 2 forks, cut butter into flour mixture until it resembles coarse crumbs. Add white chocolate and lavender, stirring until combined.
- In a liquid-measuring cup, whisk together cold cream, egg, and vanilla extract. Add to flour mixture, stirring until a dough begins to form. Working gently, bring mixture together with hands until a dough forms. (If dough seems dry and won't come together, add more cream, 1 tablespoon at a time.)
- Turn dough out onto a lightly floured surface, and knead gently until smooth by patting dough and folding it in half 4 to 5 times. Using a rolling pin, roll out dough to a ½-inch thickness. Scatter ¼ cup raspberries over half of dough. Fold other half of dough over raspberries to enclose them. Lightly roll out dough again to a ½-inch thickness. Repeat scattering, folding, and rolling process with remaining ¼ cup raspberries. Using a rolling pin, lightly roll dough to a ½-inch thickness. Using a 2-inch round cutter dipped in flour, cut 15 scones from dough, rerolling scraps as needed. Place scones 2 inches apart on prepared baking sheet.
- Sprinkle tops of scones with remaining 2 teaspoons sugar.
- Bake until edges of scones are golden brown and a wooden pick inserted in centers comes out clean, approximately 18 minutes. Let cool.
- Just before serving, place Sweetened Whipped Cream in a piping bag fitted with a large open star tip (Wilton #1M). Holding piping bag upright, pipe a rosette of whipped cream onto each scone.
- Garnish each scone with a raspberry in the center of whipped cream rosette, if desired. Serve immediately.

Sweetened Whipped Cream

Makes 3 cups

1½ cups cold heavy whipping cream
¼ cup confectioners' sugar
½ teaspoon vanilla extract

- In a deep medium bowl, beat together cold cream, confectioners' sugar, and vanilla extract with a mixer at high speed until stiff peaks form. Cover and refrigerate until ready to serve, up to 4 hours in advance.

Shrimp Salad Finger Sandwiches
Makes 12

4 cups water
3 slices lemon
2 (4-inch) sprigs fresh tarragon
¾ teaspoon kosher salt, divided
1 pound medium shrimp, peeled and deveined
½ cup mayonnaise
2 tablespoons minced celery
1 tablespoon minced fresh tarragon
1 tablespoon minced green onion
2 teaspoons fresh lemon juice
⅛ teaspoon ground black pepper
12 slices very thin white sandwich bread
Garnish: fresh tarragon sprigs

• In a medium saucepan, combine 4 cups water, lemon slices, tarragon sprigs, and ½ teaspoon salt. Bring to a boil. Remove saucepan from heat, and add shrimp. Cover and let stand for 5 minutes. Using a slotted spoon, remove shrimp from poaching liquid and place in a bowl filled with ice. Let cool completely.
• In a medium bowl, whisk together mayonnaise, celery, minced tarragon, green onion, lemon juice, black pepper, and remaining ¼ teaspoon salt.
• Remove shrimp from ice, and blot dry with paper towels. Using a sharp knife, very finely chop shrimp. Add shrimp to mayonnaise mixture, stirring until combined. Cover and refrigerate until very cold, approximately 4 hours.
• Spread a thin layer of shrimp salad onto a bread slice. Top with another bread slice, and spread with shrimp salad. Top with a third bread slice to make a triple-stack sandwich. Repeat with remaining bread slices and shrimp salad to make a total of 4 whole sandwiches.
• Using a serrated bread knife in a gentle sawing motion, trim and discard crusts from sandwiches. Cut each sandwich into 3 rectangular sandwiches. Serve immediately, or cover with damp paper towels, place in a covered container, and refrigerate for a few hours until serving time.
• Just before serving, garnish with tarragon sprigs, if desired.

Radish Flower Canapés
Makes 15

5 ounces cream cheese, softened
2½ teaspoons heavy whipping cream
1¼ teaspoons fresh lemon zest
1¼ teaspoon fresh lemon juice
¼ teaspoon fine sea salt
⅛ teaspoon ground black pepper
1 (1.9-ounce) package frozen mini phyllo shells, thawed
10 radishes

• In a medium bowl, beat together cream cheese, whipping cream, lemon zest, lemon juice, salt, and pepper at medium-low speed with a mixer until combined. Transfer cream cheese mixture to a piping bag fitted with a medium round tip (Wilton #12) or to a resealable bag with a corner snipped off. Pipe a smooth layer of cream cheese mixture into phyllo shells.
• Using a mandoline, cut 75 paper-thin slices from radishes.
• Fold each radish slice into quarters. Place 5 folded slices upright into each phyllo shell, lightly pressing into cream cheese mixture and unfolding slices slightly to resemble flower petals. Serve immediately, or refrigerate and serve within 1 hour.

Herbed Asparagus Quiches
Makes 8 (4-inch)

1 (14.1-ounce) package refrigerated piecrust
   dough (2 sheets)
8 stalks very thin asparagus
½ cup coarsely shredded Gruyère cheese
1 tablespoon chopped fresh parsley
1 tablespoon chopped fresh chives
1 tablespoon chopped fresh dill
2 large eggs
¾ cup heavy whipping cream
¼ teaspoon kosher salt
⅛ teaspoon ground black pepper

• Preheat oven to 450°. Spray 8 (3½-inch) fluted tartlet
pans with cooking spray.
• On a lightly floured surface, unfold piecrust dough.
Referring to page 133, using a 4½-inch round cutter,
cut 8 rounds from dough. Transfer rounds to prepared
tartlet pans, pressing into bottoms and up sides. Using
the wide end of a chopstick, gently press dough into
indentations in sides of pans. Trim excess dough. Using
a fork, prick bottom of dough in each tartlet pan several
times. Place tartlet pans on a rimmed baking sheet.
Freeze for 15 minutes.
• Bake until light golden brown, 7 to 9 minutes. Let cool
completely on a wire rack before filling.
• Using a sharp knife, trim and discard tough ends from
asparagus. Place asparagus on a rimmed baking sheet.
• Bake for 5 minutes, or until just crisp and tender. Cool
slightly. Using a sharp knife, coarsely chop asparagus.
• Reduce oven temperature to 350°.
• Sprinkle cheese into cooled tartlet shells. Divide
asparagus evenly among tartlet shells. Sprinkle layers
of parsley, chives, and dill evenly over asparagus.
• In a large liquid-measuring cup, whisk together eggs,
cream, salt, and pepper. Divide egg mixture evenly
among prepared tartlet shells.
• Bake until filling is set, approximately 15 minutes. Let
cool slightly on a wire rack before carefully removing
quiches from pans. Serve immediately.

*MAKE-AHEAD TIP: Quiches can be baked a day in advance,
stored in a covered container, and refrigerated. Reheat on a
rimmed baking sheet in a 350° oven, 6 to 8 minutes.*

Chocolate-Mascarpone Éclairs

Makes 30

¾ cup water
6 tablespoons unsalted butter, cubed and softened
2 teaspoons granulated sugar
¼ teaspoon fine sea salt
¾ cup all-purpose flour
3 large eggs, room temperature
Chocolate-Mascarpone Cream (recipe follows)
Bittersweet Chocolate Glaze (recipe follows)
Garnish: chopped toasted hazelnuts

• Preheat oven to 400°. Line 2 rimmed baking sheets with parchment paper.
• In a medium saucepan, combine ¾ cup water, butter, sugar, and salt. Cook over medium heat until butter melts. Add flour, stirring vigorously with a wooden spoon. Cook until dough pulls away from sides of pan, stirring constantly, 1 to 2 minutes. Remove from heat. Let stand for 2 minutes, stirring a few times to cool dough.
• Transfer dough to a large bowl. Add eggs, one at a time, beating with a mixer at medium speed until well incorporated. (Dough should be smooth and shiny.)

• Transfer dough to a piping bag fitted with a large round tip (Hobby Lobby #2A). Pipe 30 (2¾-inch) lengths of dough onto prepared baking sheets. (Pat with damp finger if dough needs additional shaping.)
• Bake for 15 minutes.
• Reduce oven temperature to 350°. Bake until éclairs are very golden brown, 20 to 25 minutes. (Insides will be dry.) Let cool completely.
• Place Chocolate-Mascarpone Cream in a piping bag fitted with a medium round tip (Wilton #12). Using a small, sharp knife, cut 2 small slits on undersides of éclairs. Pipe Chocolate-Mascarpone Cream into slits to fill éclairs.
• Dip tops of éclairs in Bittersweet Chocolate Glaze, letting excess drip off. Turn upright and sprinkle with chopped toasted hazelnuts, if desired. Serve immediately, or place in a covered container and refrigerate for up to a day.

Chocolate-Mascarpone Cream

Makes 1½ cups

1 (8-ounce) container mascarpone cheese
½ cup confectioners' sugar
2 tablespoons unsweetened cocoa powder
2 tablespoons heavy whipping cream
¼ teaspoon vanilla extract

• In a medium bowl, beat together mascarpone cheese, confectioners' sugar, cocoa powder, cream, and vanilla extract with a mixer at medium-high speed until well blended. Use immediately, or place in a covered container and refrigerate for up to a day.

Bittersweet Chocolate Glaze

Makes ⅓ cup

2 ounces bittersweet chocolate, finely chopped
¼ cup plus 2 teaspoons heavy whipping cream
1 tablespoon unsalted butter, softened

• Place chocolate in a medium bowl.
• In a small saucepan, heat cream until very hot but not boiling. Pour over chocolate. Let stand for 1 minute. Stir until smooth. Add butter, stirring until incorporated. Use immediately.

Strawberries and Cream Macarons

Makes 24

3 large egg whites
2 cups confectioners' sugar
1 cup sifted almond meal
⅛ teaspoon salt
2 tablespoons granulated sugar
1 teaspoon strawberry extract
Pink gel food coloring
Cream Cheese Filling (recipe follows)

• Place egg whites in a medium bowl, and let stand at room temperature for exactly 3 hours. (Aging egg whites in this manner is essential to creating perfect macarons.)
• Line 2 rimmed baking sheets with parchment paper. Using a pencil, draw 48 (1¼-inch) circles 2 inches apart on parchment paper. Turn parchment over.
• In a large bowl, sift together confectioners' sugar, almond meal, and salt.
• Beat egg whites with a mixer at medium-high speed until foamy, approximately 5 minutes. Gradually add granulated sugar, strawberry extract, and desired amount of food coloring, beating at high speed until stiff peaks form, 3 to 5 minutes. (Egg white mixture will be thick, creamy, and shiny.) Gently fold in almond meal mixture into egg mixture. Let batter stand for 15 minutes.
• Transfer batter to a piping bag fitted with a medium round tip (Wilton #12), and pipe batter onto drawn circles on prepared baking sheets. Tap baking sheets on counter 5 to 7 times to release air bubbles. Let stand at room temperature for 1 hour before baking to help develop the macaron's signature crisp exterior when baked. (Macarons should feel dry to the touch and not stick to the finger.)
• Preheat oven to 275°.
• Bake until macarons are firm to the touch, approximately 20 minutes. Let cool completely on pans. Remove from pans, and place in airtight containers with layers separated by wax paper. Refrigerate for up to 3 days until ready to fill and serve.
• Place Cream Cheese Filling in a piping bag fitted with a medium round tip (Wilton #12). Pipe filling onto flat side of 24 macarons, and top with remaining macarons, flat sides together. Lightly push down and twist so filling spreads to edges. Serve immediately.

Cream Cheese Filling

Makes 1½ cups

½ cup unsalted butter, softened
4 ounces cream cheese, softened
2 cups confectioners' sugar
¼ teaspoon fine sea salt

• In a large bowl, beat together butter, cream cheese, confectioners' sugar, and salt with a mixer at high speed until light and fluffy. Use immediately, or place in a covered container, refrigerate, and use within 3 days. Let come to room temperature before using.

- Preheat oven to 350°. Line a 24-well muffin pan with paper cupcake liners.
- In a large bowl, beat together butter and sugar with a mixer at medium speed until light and fluffy, 3 to 4 minutes.
- In a medium bowl, whisk together flour, baking powder, and salt.
- In a small bowl, stir together milk, crème fraîche, almond extract, and vanilla extract. Gradually add flour mixture to butter mixture, alternately with milk mixture, beginning and ending with flour mixture, beating at low speed just until combined after each addition.
- In another large bowl, using clean beaters, beat egg whites with a mixer at high speed until stiff peaks form. Stir a fourth of beaten egg whites into batter. Using a rubber spatula, gently fold remainder of egg whites into batter. Spoon batter into prepared muffin cups, filling halfway.
- Bake until a wooden pick inserted in centers of cupcakes comes out clean, 15 to 18 minutes. Let cool in pan for 5 minutes. Transfer cupcakes to a wire rack. Let cool completely.
- Place Crème Fraîche Buttercream in a piping bag fitted with a large open star tip (Wilton #1M). Pipe buttercream onto cupcakes.
- Garnish with sprinkles, if desired. Place decorative wrappers* around cupcakes before serving, if desired.

*We used Celebrate It Gold Glitter Cupcake Wrappers, available at Michaels, 800-642-4235, michaels.com.

Almond–Crème Fraîche Cupcakes
Makes 24

1 cup unsalted butter, softened
2 cups granulated sugar
3¾ cups cake flour
2½ teaspoons baking powder
½ teaspoon fine sea salt
¾ cup plus 2 tablespoons whole milk
¼ cup crème fraîche
½ teaspoon almond extract
¼ teaspoon vanilla extract
4 large egg whites, room temperature
Crème Fraîche Buttercream (recipe follows)
Garnish: heart-shaped and glitter sprinkles

Crème Fraîche Buttercream
Makes 3¾ cups

1½ cups unsalted butter, softened
7½ cups confectioners' sugar
¾ teaspoon fine sea salt
¾ teaspoon vanilla extract
¼ teaspoon almond extract
1 cup crème fraîche

- In a large bowl, beat together butter, confectioners' sugar, salt, vanilla extract, and almond extract with a mixer at high speed until light and fluffy. Add crème fraîche, beating at medium speed just until incorporated. Use immediately.

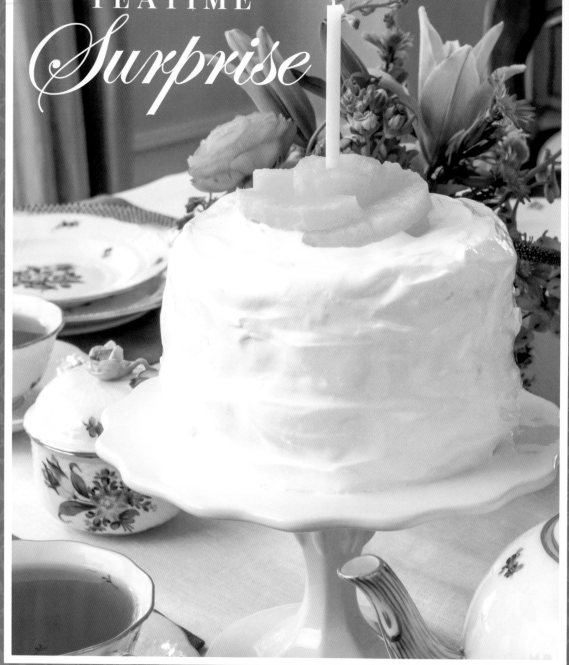

TEATIME *Surprise*

The
MENU

SCONE
Apricot Scones
Cardamom Black Tea

SAVORIES
Roast Beef Tea Sandwiches
Ruffled Cucumber Canapés
Green Olive–Shrimp Salad
Canapés
Chun Mee Leaf Green Tea

SWEETS
Walnut-Thyme Tea Cakes
Chocolate-Mascarpone Tartlets
Pineapple-Filled White Layer Cake
*Strawberry Velvet Cake
Dessert Tea*

Tea Pairings by Ahmad Tea
800-637-7704 • ahmadteausa.com

*The unsuspecting guest
of honor will be charmed
with a teatime jubilee
that concludes with a
delectable fruit-filled
birthday cake.*

Apricot Scones
Makes 12

2 cups all-purpose flour
¼ cup plus 1 teaspoon granulated sugar, divided
2 teaspoons baking powder
½ teaspoon salt
4 tablespoons cold unsalted butter, cubed
½ cup chopped dried apricots
¾ cup plus 3 tablespoons cold heavy whipping cream, divided
½ teaspoon vanilla extract

• Preheat oven to 350°.
• Line a rimmed baking sheet with parchment paper.
• In a large bowl, whisk together flour, ¼ cup sugar, baking powder, and salt. Using a pastry blender or 2 forks, cut cold butter into flour mixture until it resembles coarse crumbs. Stir in apricots.
• In a small bowl, whisk together ¾ cup plus 2 tablespoons cold cream and vanilla extract. Add to flour mixture, stirring until a dough begins to form. Working gently, bring mixture together with hands until a dough forms. (If dough seems dry, add more cream, 1 tablespoon at a time.)
• Turn out dough onto a lightly floured surface, and knead gently until smooth by patting dough and folding it in half 4 to 5 times. Using a rolling pin, roll dough to a ¾-inch thickness. Using a 2-inch fluted square cutter dipped in flour, cut 12 scones from dough. Place scones 2 inches apart on prepared baking sheet.
• Brush tops of scones with remaining 1 tablespoon cream, and sprinkle with remaining 1 teaspoon sugar.
• Bake until edges of scones are golden brown and a wooden pick inserted in the centers comes out clean, approximately 20 minutes. Serve warm.

RECOMMENDED CONDIMENTS:
Clotted Cream
Orange Marmalade

"Count your age by friends, not years.
Count your life by smiles, not tears." —1927 BIRTHDAY CARD

Roast Beef Tea Sandwiches
Makes 12

6 slices potato bread
Horseradish Aïoli (recipe follows)
12 slices ultra-thin deli-style roast beef
12 slices Campari tomato
Garnish: microgreens

• Using a long serrated knife, trim crusts from bread, and cut each bread slice diagonally into 4 triangles. To prevent drying out, cover bread with damp paper towels, or place in a resealable plastic bag until ready to assemble sandwiches.
• Spread a small amount of Horseradish Aïoli onto each bread triangle.
• Fold each roast beef slice in half, then in half again to create a ruffled triangle. Place a roast beef triangle on aïoli side of 12 bread triangles. Top each with a tomato slice and another bread triangle, aïoli side down.
• Garnish with microgreens, if desired. Serve immediately.

MAKE-AHEAD TIP: Sandwiches can be made in advance without the tomato slices or garnish, covered with damp paper towels, placed in an airtight container, and refrigerated for up to 4 hours. Insert tomato slices, and garnish with microgreens just before serving.

Horseradish Aïoli
Makes ¼ cup

2 tablespoons mayonnaise
2 tablespoons sour cream
1 tablespoon prepared grated horseradish
⅛ teaspoon ground black pepper

• In a small bowl, stir together mayonnaise, sour cream, horseradish, and pepper. Use immediately, or cover and refrigerate for up to a day.

Ruffled Cucumber Canapés
Makes 6

1½ English cucumbers
6 slices very thin white bread
Pink Peppercorn Butter (recipe follows)
Garnish: ground pink peppercorns

• Cut cucumbers in half lengthwise.
• Using a long serrated bread knife in a gentle sawing motion, trim crusts from bread slices and cut each bread slice to the same width as the cucumber halves. Discard bread scraps.
• Cut cucumber halves into 5-inch lengths. Using a mandoline, cut 24 paper-thin slices from cucumber lengths, and arrange on paper towels to absorb moisture.
• Spread a thin layer of Pink Peppercorn Butter onto each bread slice. Place a cucumber slice on a bread rectangle, rolling back top edge and looping cucumber slice. Fold a cucumber slice in half to make a loop, and place on top of first looped slice in a staggered fashion. Add 2 more slices in the same manner. With the last cucumber slice, finish off by rolling end forward and back and tucking under. Repeat for remaining bread rectangles and cucumber slices.
• Garnish with a sprinkle of ground peppercorns, if desired.

MAKE-AHEAD TIP: Canapés can be assembled an hour in advance, covered with damp paper towels, and refrigerated until serving time.

Pink Peppercorn Butter
Makes ¼ cup

4 tablespoons salted butter, softened
¼ teaspoon ground pink peppercorns

• In a small bowl, combine butter and pink peppercorns, stirring to blend.

Green Olive–Shrimp Salad Canapés

Makes 12

1 pound headless shrimp, peeled, deveined,
  and cooked
3 tablespoons mayonnaise
2 tablespoons finely chopped Castelvetrano
  green olives
2 tablespoons finely chopped celery
1 tablespoon finely chopped green onion
  (green tops only)
2 teaspoons fresh lemon juice
½ teaspoon salt-free herb-and-spice seasoning blend*
¼ teaspoon salt
⅛ teaspoon ground black pepper
4 slices firm white sandwich bread, frozen
Garnish: 12 lemon curls**

• In the work bowl of a food processor, pulse shrimp
until finely chopped.
• In a bowl, stir together shrimp, mayonnaise, olives,
celery, green onion, lemon juice, seasoning blend, salt,
and pepper. Cover, and refrigerate until cold, approximately 4 hours.
• Using a 2-inch round cutter, cut 12 shapes from frozen
bread, discarding scraps. Place bread rounds in a resealable plastic bag until bread has thawed.
• Place a scoop of cold shrimp salad on each thawed
bread round.
• Garnish each canapé with a lemon curl, if desired.
Serve immediately.

We used Mrs. Dash Original Blend.
**Using a channel knife or a zesting tool, cut long strips of lemon
peel. Wrap strips around a straw to shape. Using kitchen shears,
cut curled peel to desired lengths. Use immediately.*

Walnut-Thyme Tea Cakes
Makes approximately 22

½ cup unsalted butter, softened
½ cup confectioners' sugar, divided
½ teaspoon vanilla extract
1 cup all-purpose flour
¼ teaspoon salt
½ cup very finely chopped toasted walnuts
1 teaspoon finely chopped fresh thyme leaves
Garnish: additional confectioners' sugar and
   fresh thyme sprigs

• Preheat oven to 325°. Line 2 baking sheets with
parchment paper.
• In a large bowl, beat butter at medium speed with a
mixer until smooth and creamy. Add ¼ cup confectioners' sugar and vanilla extract, beating until light and
creamy. Add flour and salt, stirring until well combined.
Add walnuts and thyme, stirring well.
• Using a levered 2-teaspoon scoop, drop dough 1 inch
apart onto prepared baking sheets.
• Bake until edges of tea cakes are light brown, approximately 14 minutes. Transfer to wire cooling racks, and
sprinkle with remaining ¼ cup confectioners' sugar.
Let cool completely. Store in an airtight container with
wax paper between layers.
• Just before serving, garnish with an additional dusting
of confectioners' sugar. Garnish each tea cake with a
fresh thyme sprig, if desired.

Chocolate-Mascarpone Tartlets

Makes 24

1 (4-ounce) semisweet chocolate baking bar
1 (8-ounce) container mascarpone cheese
1 tablespoon confectioners' sugar
1 tablespoon heavy whipping cream
½ teaspoon vanilla extract
⅛ teaspoon salt
24 Mini Tartlet Shells (recipe follows) or mini prepared
   shortbread tartlet shells
Garnish: 24 mini kiwi slices

• Melt chocolate according to package directions.
Let cool slightly.
• In a medium bowl, combine mascarpone cheese,
confectioners' sugar, cream, vanilla extract, and salt,
stirring well to blend. Add melted chocolate, stirring
until incorporated.
• Transfer chocolate mixture to a piping bag fitted with
a large open-star tip (Wilton #1M). Pipe rosettes of
chocolate mixture into tartlet shells.
• Garnish each tartlet with a mini kiwi slice, if desired.

Mini Tartlet Shells

Makes 24 (1¾-inch)

2¼ cups all-purpose flour
6 tablespoons granulated sugar
3 tablespoons confectioners' sugar
⅜ teaspoon salt
½ cup plus 7 tablespoons very cold unsalted butter,
   cut into cubes
1½ tablespoons very cold water
1½ tablespoons unsalted butter, softened

• Spray 24 (1¾-inch) tartlet pans* lightly with baking
spray. Place tartlet pans on a rimmed baking sheet.
• In the work bowl of a food processor, pulse together
flour, granulated sugar, confectioners' sugar, and salt
until blended. Add cold butter, pulsing until it resembles
peas. Add 1½ tablespoons very cold water, pulsing until
a dough forms.
• Turn out dough onto a lightly floured surface, and
shape into a disk. Wrap dough securely in plastic wrap,
and refrigerate for at least 30 minutes.
• Preheat oven to 350°.
• Unwrap and place dough on a lightly floured surface.
Using a rolling pin, roll dough to a ¼-inch thickness.
Referring to page 133, using a 2½-inch round cutter,

cut 24 rounds from dough, rerolling scraps once. Being
careful not to stretch dough, center a dough round atop
each prepared tartlet pan. Lightly press dough rounds
into bottoms of tartlet pans, and stand dough up against
sides of pans. Using a rolling pin, roll over tops of tartlet
pans to trim excess dough. Using large end of a chopstick, press dough into indentations in sides of tartlet
pans. Place tartlet pans in freezer for 15 minutes.
• Coat a 12x8-inch piece of foil with softened butter.
Cut foil into 24 (2-inch) squares. Place a foil square,
butter side down, in center of each prepared tartlet pan,
and place ceramic pie weights or dried beans atop each
foil square.
• Bake for 10 minutes. Carefully remove pie weights and
foil. Using a fork, prick bottoms of tartlet shells.
• Bake until light golden brown, 5 to 10 minutes. Let
cool completely before carefully removing tartlet shells
from pans. Use immediately, or store at room temperature in an airtight container for up to a day.

*We recommend Ateco 4840 Tartlet Forms.

Pineapple-Filled White Layer Cake

Makes 1 (6-inch) cake, approximately 8 servings

4 tablespoons unsalted butter, softened
½ cup plus 2 tablespoons granulated sugar, divided
½ teaspoon vanilla extract
1 cup cake flour
1 teaspoon baking powder
¼ teaspoon salt
6 tablespoons whole milk
3 large egg whites, room temperature
Pineapple Filling (recipe follows)
Fluffy White Frosting (recipe follows)
Garnish: 1 (8-ounce) can pineapple slices, drained

• Preheat oven to 350°. Spray 3 (6-inch) round cake pans with baking spray with flour.
• In a large bowl, beat together butter and ½ cup sugar with a mixer at high speed until light and fluffy, approximately 5 minutes. Add vanilla extract, beating to combine.
• In a medium bowl, whisk together flour, baking powder, and salt. Add to butter mixture in thirds, alternately with milk, beginning and ending with flour mixture.
• In another medium mixing bowl, beat egg whites with a mixer at high speed until frothy. Slowly add remaining 2 tablespoons sugar, continuing to beat until soft peaks form. Gently fold egg whites into cake batter until incorporated.

• Divide batter evenly among prepared cake pans. Using an offset spatula, smooth batter in pans.
• Bake until edges of cake layers are golden brown and a wooden pick inserted in centers comes out clean, approximately 13 minutes. Let cake layers cool in pans for 10 minutes. Invert onto wire cooling racks, and let cool completely.
• Place a cake layer on a cake plate, and spread layer with half of Pineapple Filling. Top with another cake layer, and spread with remaining half of filling. Top with remaining cake layer.
• Refrigerate cake until filling is firm, approximately 1 hour.
• Using an offset spatula to create decorative swirls, spread Fluffy White Frosting over sides and top of cake.
• Garnish top of cake by cutting pineapple slices into halves or thirds and arranging in overlapping concentric circles to resemble a flower, if desired.

Pineapple Filling

Makes ¾ cup

1 (8.25-ounce) can crushed pineapple in heavy syrup
1 tablespoon granulated sugar
1 tablespoon cornstarch
⅛ teaspoon salt
1 tablespoon unsalted butter
¼ teaspoon vanilla extract

• In a medium saucepan, combine pineapple with syrup, sugar, cornstarch, and salt. Cook over medium heat until mixture begins to simmer. Reduce heat to low, and cook for 3 minutes.
• Remove from heat, and add butter and vanilla extract, stirring until butter melts.

Fluffy White Frosting

Makes 2 cups

½ cup plus 3 tablespoons granulated sugar
¼ teaspoon cream of tartar
⅛ teaspoon salt
3 tablespoons water
1 egg white, room temperature

• In the top half of a double boiler set over simmering water, combine sugar, cream of tartar, salt, water, and egg white. (Do not let bottom of bowl touch water.) Beat with a mixer at high speed until frosting thickens and forms stiff peaks, 7 to 10 minutes. Use immediately.

BUTTERFLY-KISSED
Birthday

The
MENU

SCONE
Golden Raisin–Tarragon Scones

*Ceylon Blackwood Estate
Organic Black Tea*

SAVORIES
Herbed Mini Patty Pan Squash

Apricot, Prosciutto, Chive &
Goat Cheese Croustades

Cucumber-Sprouts Canapés

Green Guava Blend Tea

SWEETS
Lemon-Basil French Macarons

Raspberry Tartlets

Vanilla Cupcakes with
Vanilla Bean–Browned
Butter Frosting

Creamy Toasted Coconut Oolong Tea

Tea Pairings by Simpson & Vail
800-282-8327 • svtea.com

*An alfresco afternoon
tea with butterfly-topped
cupcakes in lieu of a
traditional cake with
candles is ideal for those
born in spring or summer.*

Golden Raisin–Tarragon Scones

Makes 9

2 cups all-purpose flour
¼ cup granulated sugar
2 teaspoons baking powder
½ teaspoon salt
¼ cup cold unsalted butter, cubed
⅓ cup golden raisins
1 teaspoon finely chopped fresh tarragon
¾ cup plus 3 tablespoons cold heavy whipping cream,
    divided
¼ teaspoon vanilla extract
Garnish: fresh blueberries, fresh blackberries,
    fresh tarragon, and fresh edible flowers*

• Preheat oven to 350°. Line a rimmed baking sheet with
parchment paper.
• In a large bowl, whisk together flour, sugar, baking
powder, and salt. Using a pastry blender or 2 forks, cut in
cold butter until it resembles coarse crumbs. Add raisins
and tarragon, stirring to combine.
• In a small bowl, stir together ¾ cup plus 2 tablespoons
cold cream and vanilla extract. Add cream mixture to
flour mixture, stirring until a dough begins to form.
Working gently, bring mixture together with hands until
a dough forms. (If dough seems dry, add more cream,
1 tablespoon at a time.)
• Turn out dough onto a lightly floured surface, and
knead gently until smooth by patting dough and folding
it in half 5 to 7 times. Using a rolling pin, roll out dough
to a 1-inch thickness. Using a 2¼-inch fluted round
cutter dipped in flour, cut 9 scones from dough. Place
scones 2 inches apart on prepared baking sheet. Brush
tops of scones with remaining 1 tablespoon cream.
• Bake until edges of scones are golden brown and
wooden pick inserted in centers comes out clean,
approximately 20 minutes.
• Garnish with blueberries, blackberries, tarragon, and
edible flowers, if desired.

*Edible flowers are available from Gourmet Sweet Botanicals,
800-931-7530, gourmetsweetbotanicals.com.*

RECOMMENDED CONDIMENTS:
Devonshire Cream
Lemon Curd

Herbed Mini Patty Pan Squash

Makes 12

12 yellow mini patty pan squash
¼ cup panko (Japanese bread crumbs)
¼ cup grated Parmesan cheese
2 tablespoons unsalted butter, melted
¼ teaspoon fresh thyme leaves
⅛ teaspoon garlic powder
⅛ teaspoon salt
⅛ teaspoon ground black pepper
Garnish: paprika

• Preheat oven to 400°. Line a rimmed baking sheet with foil.
• Using a sharp paring knife, trim bottoms of squash to sit level. Cut off tops. Using a melon baller, scoop out and discard insides of squash. Place squash shells on prepared baking sheet.
• In a small bowl, stir together bread crumbs, cheese, melted butter, thyme, garlic powder, salt, and pepper until well combined. Spoon mixture into squash shells.
• Bake until squash are tender when pierced with the tip of a sharp knife and bread crumbs are golden, 8 to 10 minutes.
• Garnish with paprika, if desired. Serve warm or at room temperature.

Apricot, Prosciutto, Chive & Goat Cheese Croustades

Makes 12

4 ounces goat cheese, softened
1 tablespoon heavy whipping cream
½ teaspoon finely chopped fresh chives
⅛ teaspoon ground black pepper
12 croustade shells*
12 very thin slices prosciutto
Apricot Chutney (recipe follows)
Garnish: finely chopped fresh chives

• In a small bowl, stir together goat cheese, cream, chives, and pepper. Transfer goat cheese mixture to a piping bag fitted with a large closed star tip (Wilton #2D).
• Pipe a dollop of goat cheese mixture into bottom of each croustade shell, leaving room for additional ingredients. Place 1 prosciutto slice in each croustade, ruffling to fit. Pipe another dollop of goat cheese mixture onto

prosciutto. Top with a small amount of Apricot Chutney.
• Garnish with chives, if desired. Serve immediately.

We used Siljans.

Apricot Chutney

Makes ¼ cup

¼ cup finely chopped dried apricots
2 tablespoons sherry vinegar
1 tablespoon granulated sugar

• In a small saucepan, bring apricots, vinegar, and sugar to a boil over medium-high heat. Reduce heat, and simmer until apricots are softened and mixture is slightly thickened, 3 to 5 minutes. Let cool slightly before using, or cover and refrigerate for up to a day.

Cucumber-Sprouts Canapés

Makes 12

3 large slices firm white sandwich bread, frozen
Lemon-Pepper Aïoli (recipe follows)
1 English cucumber
⅓ cup alfalfa sprouts

• Using a 2-inch square cutter, cut 12 shapes from frozen bread, discarding scraps. Place bread squares in a resealable plastic bag, and let thaw at room temperature.
• Spread a layer of Lemon-Peppper Aïoli onto each bread square.
• Using a mandoline or a sharp paring knife, cut 60 paper-thin slices from cucumber.
• Place 5 cucumber slices on aïoli side of each bread square, layering in an overlapping circle. Top each with alfalfa sprouts. Serve immediately.

Lemon-Pepper Aïoli

Makes ¼ cup

¼ cup mayonnaise
½ teaspoon fresh lemon zest
⅛ teaspoon ground black pepper

• In a small bowl, stir together mayonnaise, lemon zest, and pepper. Use immediately, or cover and refrigerate for up to a day.

• In the bowl of a stand mixer fitted with the whisk attachment, beat egg whites at medium-high speed until thick, shiny, and creamy, approximately 5 minutes. Add lemon extract and desired amount of food coloring, beating until combined. Using a large spatula, fold in almond meal mixture until batter falls in thick ribbons. Let batter stand for 15 minutes.
• Transfer batter to a piping bag fitted with a medium round tip (Wilton #12). Pipe batter into drawn circles on prepared baking sheet. Tap pans vigorously on counter 5 to 7 times to release air bubbles. Let stand at room temperature for 45 to 60 minutes before baking to help develop the macaron's signature crisp exterior when baked. (Macarons should feel dry to the touch and should not stick to finger.)
• Preheat oven to 275°.
• Bake until macarons are firm to the touch, approximately 20 minutes. Let cool completely on pans.
• Transfer macarons to an airtight container with layers separated by wax paper. Refrigerate until ready to serve.
• Place Basil-Lemon Cream Cheese Filling in a piping bag fitted with a medium round tip (Wilton #12). Pipe filling onto flat side of half of macarons. Place remaining macarons, flat side down, on top of filling. Lightly push down so filling spreads to edges. Serve immediately.

We used Wilton.

MAKE-AHEAD TIP: *Wrap unfilled macarons in plastic wrap in groups to prevent crushing or breaking. Transfer to airtight containers. Refrigerate for up to 2 days until needed. Let come to room temperature before filling and serving.*

Basil-Lemon Cream Cheese Filling
Makes 1 cup

1 (8-ounce) package cream cheese, softened
2 tablespoons confectioners' sugar
1 teaspoon fresh lemon zest
Leaf-green paste food coloring*
1 tablespoon finely chopped fresh basil

• In a medium bowl, beat together cream cheese, confectioners' sugar, and lemon zest with a mixer at medium speed until light and creamy. Add desired amount of food coloring, beating until combined. Add basil, beating until combined. Use immediately.

Lemon-Basil French Macarons
Makes 19

3 large egg whites
2 cups confectioners' sugar
1 cup sifted almond meal
⅛ teaspoon salt
1 tablespoon granulated sugar
¼ teaspoon lemon extract
Lemon-yellow paste food coloring*
Basil-Lemon Cream Cheese Filling (recipe follows)

• Place egg whites in a medium bowl, and let stand at room temperature for exactly 3 hours. (Aging the egg whites in this manner is essential to creating perfect macarons.)
• Line 2 rimmed baking sheets with parchment paper. Using a pencil, draw 38 (1¾-inch) circles 2 inches apart onto parchment; turn parchment over.
• In the work bowl of a food processor, pulse together confectioners' sugar, almond meal, and salt just to combine.

Raspberry Tartlets

Makes 6

½ cup water
½ cup orange juice
¼ cup granulated sugar
2 tablespoons fresh lemon juice
1 tablespoon cornstarch
⅛ teaspoon salt
3 cups fresh raspberries, divided
6 Tartlet Shells (recipe follows)

• In a medium saucepan, whisk together ½ cup water, orange juice, sugar, lemon juice, cornstarch, and salt until well combined. Bring to a boil over medium-high heat, whisking constantly. Add 1 cup raspberries, and cook over medium heat, stirring frequently, until raspberries have fallen apart and mixture has thickened slightly, 5 to 7 minutes. Strain mixture through a fine-mesh sieve into a heatproof bowl, and let cool to room temperature.
• Arrange remaining 2 cups raspberries in an upright position in Tartlet Shells. Pour cooled raspberry glaze over raspberries, filling shells. Refrigerate until filling sets, approximately 1 hour.

Tartlet Shells

Makes 6

1½ cups all-purpose flour
¼ cup granulated sugar
2 tablespoons confectioners' sugar
¼ teaspoon salt
10 tablespoons very cold unsalted butter, cubed
1 tablespoon very cold water
1 tablespoon unsalted butter, softened

• Spray 6 (3½-inch) tartlet pans* lightly with baking spray with flour. Place tartlet pans on a rimmed baking sheet.
• In the work bowl of a food processor, place flour, granulated sugar, confectioners' sugar, and salt; pulse to blend. Add cold butter, pulsing until it resembles peas. Add 1 tablespoon very cold water, pulsing until a dough forms.
• Turn out dough onto a lightly floured surface, and shape into a disk. Wrap tightly in plastic wrap, and refrigerate for at least 30 minutes.

• Preheat oven to 375°.
• Turn out dough onto a lightly floured surface. Using a rolling pin, roll out dough to a ¼-inch thickness. Referring to page 133, using a 4½-inch round cutter, cut 6 rounds from dough, rerolling scraps once. Being careful not to stretch dough, center a dough round atop each prepared tartlet pan. Lightly press dough rounds into bottoms of tartlet pans, and stand dough up against sides of pans. Using a rolling pin, roll over tops of tartlet pans to trim excess dough. Using the large end of a chopstick, press dough into indentations in sides of tartlet pans. Place tartlet pans in freezer for 15 minutes.
• Coat a 9x6-inch piece of foil with softened butter. Cut foil into 6 (3-inch) squares. Place a foil square, butter side down, in center of each prepared tartlet pan, and place ceramic pie weights or dried beans atop each foil square.
• Bake for 10 minutes. Carefully remove foil and weights. Using a fork, prick bottom of tartlet shells.
• Bake until shells are light golden brown, approximately 15 minutes. Let cool completely before carefully removing tartlet shells from pans. Use immediately, or store at room temperature in an airtight container for up to a day.

We recommend Gobel 3.5-inch nonstick tartlet pans, available from Sur la Table, 800-243-0852, surlatable.com.

- Divide batter among prepared muffin cups. Tap pan on counter to level batter and reduce air bubbles.
- Bake until a wooden pick inserted in centers comes out clean, approximately 17 minutes. Let cool completely in pan on a wire rack.
- Remove cupcakes from pan, and place in decorative cupcake wrappers, if desired.
- Place Vanilla Bean–Browned Butter Frosting in a piping bag fitted with large open star tip (Wilton #1M), and pipe a decorative swirl on top of cupcakes.
- Garnish with edible wafer paper butterflies, if desired.

Wafer paper butterflies and butterfly cupcake wrappers are available from Fancy Flours, 406-587-0118, fancyflours.com. Follow directions given for brushing wafer paper butterflies with corn syrup and letting dry before serving.

Vanilla Bean–Browned Butter Frosting
Makes 4½ cups

1½ cups unsalted butter, softened
5 cups confectioners' sugar
2 vanilla beans, split lengthwise, seeds scraped and reserved
1½ teaspoons fine sea salt*
2½ tablespoons whole milk
2 teaspoons heavy whipping cream

- In a medium saucepan, melt butter over medium-high heat until it foams. Using a rubber spatula, scrape bottom of pan to keep butter from burning so it will brown evenly. (Reduce heat, if necessary.) Let butter foam a second time. Stir, watching carefully so butter does not burn, until butter is a deep golden yellow and has a nutty aroma.
- Transfer browned butter to a heatproof bowl, and let cool to room temperature. Refrigerate until butter becomes solid but not hard.
- In a large bowl, beat chilled browned butter with a mixer at medium speed for 2 minutes. Add confectioners' sugar, beating at low speed until fluffy. Add reserved vanilla bean seeds and salt, beating to combine. Add milk and cream, beating at high speed until frosting is light and fluffy. Use immediately.

Fine sea salt is important to use for the taste and texture of this frosting. Don't substitute another salt. If a sweeter, less salty frosting is desired, reduce amount of salt.

Vanilla Cupcakes with Vanilla Bean–Browned Butter Frosting
Makes 12

½ cup unsalted butter, softened
⅔ cup granulated sugar
3 large eggs
1½ teaspoons vanilla extract
½ teaspoon butter extract
1½ cups all-purpose flour
1½ teaspoons baking powder
¼ teaspoon salt
¼ cup whole milk
Vanilla Bean–Browned Butter Frosting (recipe follows)
Garnish: decorative cupcake wrappers and edible wafer paper butterflies*

- Preheat oven to 350°. Line a 12-well muffin pan with cupcake liners.
- In a large bowl, beat together butter and sugar with a mixer at medium speed until fluffy, 3 to 4 minutes, stopping to scrape sides of bowl. Add eggs, one at a time, beating well after each addition. Add vanilla extract and butter extract, beating until incorporated.
- In a medium bowl, whisk together flour, baking powder, and salt. With mixer at low speed, gradually add flour mixture to butter mixture alternately with milk, beginning and ending with flour mixture, beating just until combined after each addition.

A GRAND
Occasion

The
MENU

SCONE
Walnut-Ginger Scones
Cream Earl Grey Black Tea

SAVORIES
Roasted Mushroom Frico Cups
Beef Filet Tea Sandwiches
Olive–Cream Cheese
Cucumber Sandwiches
Apricot Oolong Tea

SWEETS
Fruit-Topped
Vanilla Panna Cottas
Lacy Pecan Cookies
Cardamom-Orange Cakes with
Browned Butter Frosting
Mango Strawberry Heaven Rooibos

Tea Pairings by True Leaf Tea Company
713-218-6300 • trueleaftea.com

Invite beloved companions to
an elegant birthday celebration
at a table set with cheery
blossoms and cherished china
for afternoon tea.

Walnut-Ginger Scones

Makes 11

2½ cups all-purpose flour
⅓ cup granulated sugar
1 tablespoon baking powder
½ teaspoon salt
4 tablespoons cold unsalted butter, cubed
½ cup chopped toasted walnuts
¼ cup chopped crystallized ginger
1 cup plus 2 tablespoons cold heavy cream, divided
½ teaspoon vanilla extract
Garnish: cane sugar

• Preheat oven to 375°. Line a rimmed baking sheet with parchment paper.
• In a large bowl, whisk together flour, sugar, baking powder, and salt. Using a pastry blender or 2 forks, cut cold butter into flour mixture until it resembles coarse crumbs. Add walnuts and ginger, stirring until incorporated.
• In a small bowl, stir together 1 cup plus 1 tablespoon cold cream and vanilla extract. Add cream mixture to flour mixture, stirring until a dough begins to form. Working gently, bring mixture together with hands until a dough forms. (If mixture seems dry and dough won't come together, add more cream, 1 tablespoon at a time.)
• Turn out dough onto a lightly floured surface, and knead gently 3 to 4 times. Using a rolling pin, roll out dough out to a 1-inch thickness. Using a 2-inch fluted round cutter dipped in flour, cut 11 scones from dough, rerolling scraps as needed. Place scones 2 inches apart on prepared baking sheet.
• Brush tops of scones with remaining 1 tablespoon cream. Garnish with a sprinkle of cane sugar, if desired.
• Bake until edges of scones are golden brown and a wooden pick inserted in centers comes out clean, 20 to 22 minutes. Serve warm.

RECOMMENDED CONDIMENTS:

Devonshire Cream
Lemon Curd

Roasted Mushroom Frico Cups

Makes 6

8 ounces gourmet blend fresh mushrooms
⅓ cup thinly sliced shallots
2 tablespoons extra-virgin olive oil, divided
1 teaspoon fresh thyme leaves
¼ teaspoon salt
¼ teaspoon ground black pepper
¼ cup coarsely chopped baby arugula
1 tablespoon finely chopped fresh parsley
1 tablespoon red wine vinegar
6 Parmesan Frico Cups (recipe follows)
Garnish: fresh thyme sprig

• Preheat oven to 350°. Line a rimmed baking sheet with foil.
• In a large bowl, toss together mushrooms, shallots, 1 tablespoon olive oil, thyme, salt, and pepper until coated. Spread mushrooms in an even layer on prepared baking sheet.
• Bake until mushrooms are tender and have released their juices, 18 to 20 minutes. Let cool completely. Transfer cooled mushrooms to a cutting board.
• Using a sharp knife, coarsely chop mushrooms. Transfer mushrooms to a large bowl. Add arugula and parsley, stirring to combine. Just before serving, divide mushroom mixture among Parmesan Frico Cups.
• In a small liquid-measuring cup, whisk together vinegar and remaining 1 tablespoon olive oil. Immediately drizzle over mushroom mixture.
• Garnish with a fresh thyme sprig, if desired.

Parmesan Frico Cups

Makes 6

1½ cups pre-shredded Parmesan cheese

• Preheat oven to 350°. Line 2 rimmed baking sheets with parchment paper or silicone baking mats. Invert a mini muffin pan.
• Working with 1 baking sheet at a time, sprinkle ¾ cup cheese in an even layer in 3 (3½-inch) circles (¼ cup cheese per circle) on each prepared baking sheet.
• Bake until cheese melts and is golden brown around edges, 5 to 7 minutes.
• Using a thin metal spatula and working carefully and quickly, drape each cheese circle over back of prepared mini muffin pan, forming a ruffled cup. Let cool completely. Store in an airtight container and use within 8 hours.

Beef Filet Tea Sandwiches

Makes 6

1 (6-ounce) beef tenderloin filet steak
1 tablespoon extra-virgin olive oil
⅛ teaspoon garlic salt
⅛ teaspoon ground black pepper
6 slices soft Italian bread*
Blue Cheese Aïoli (recipe follows)
18 spinach leaves
6 slices Campari tomato
6 pieced cooked bacon

• Coat both sides of beef filet with olive oil. Sprinkle with garlic salt and pepper, rubbing spices into meat. Let come to room temperature.
• Preheat a small cast-iron skillet or heavy-bottomed pan over medium-high heat.
• Add filet to hot skillet. Reduce heat to medium, and let cook for 7 to 9 minutes per side—longer for well-done beef. Remove filet from pan and let rest for 10 minutes. Using a sharp knife, cut filet into 6 thin slices, and cut slices into 2¾x1½-inch rectangles. Blot well on paper towels before using.
• Using a serrated bread knife in a gentle sawing motion, trim and discard crusts from bread slices, and cut 12 (2¾x1½-inch) rectangles from bread slices. Spread a layer of Blue Cheese Aïoli onto bread rectangles. On aïoli side of 6 bread rectangles, layer on each 3 spinach leaves, 1 beef rectangle, 1 tomato slice, and 1 bacon piece. Cover each with a remaining bread rectangle, aïoli side down. Serve immediately, or cover with damp paper towels and serve within 1 hour.

We used Arnold Italian Bread.

MAKE-AHEAD TIP: Beef may be cooked one day in advance, wrapped well, and refrigerated. Slice and serve cold, if desired.

Blue Cheese Aïoli

Makes approximately ½ cup

⅓ cup mayonnaise
3 tablespoons blue cheese crumbles
⅛ teaspoon ground black pepper

• In a small bowl, stir together mayonnaise, blue cheese, and pepper until combined. Use immediately, or transfer to an airtight container, refrigerate, and use within a day.

Olive–Cream Cheese Cucumber Sandwiches

Makes 6

6 slices very thin white bread, frozen
2 ounces cream cheese, softened
2 tablespoons finely chopped Castelvetrano olives
½ teaspoon fresh lemon zest
½ teaspoon fresh lemon juice
⅛ teaspoon salt
⅛ teaspoon ground black pepper
36 paper-thin slices English cucumber

• Using a 1½-inch square cutter, cut 12 squares from frozen bread, discarding scraps. Keep covered with a damp paper towel or place in a resealable plastic bag to maintain freshness and let thaw.

• In a small bowl, stir together cream cheese, olives, lemon zest, lemon juice, salt, and pepper. Spread an even layer of olive mixture onto bread squares.
• Place 1 cucumber slice on olive side of 1 bread square. Top with another bread square, olive side up. Fold a cucumber slice in half, and then in half again to form a flower petal. Place folded cucumber slice on top of bread square, pressing into olive mixture to adhere. Repeat with 4 cucumber slices to make a flower shape. Repeat with remaining ingredients to make 5 more cucumber flower–topped sandwiches. Serve immediately, or place in a container, lightly cover with damp paper towels, and refrigerate for up to 1 hour.

KITCHEN TIP: Blot cucumber slices on paper towels to absorb excess moisture before folding into flowers.

Fruit-Topped Vanilla Panna Cottas
Makes 6 (⅓-cup) servings

1 (.25-ounce) envelope plain gelatin
¼ cup water
2 cups heavy whipping cream
⅓ cup granulated sugar
¾ teaspoon vanilla extract
Garnish: fresh raspberries, blueberries, blackberries,
    and mint sprigs

• In a small bowl, stir together gelatin and ¼ cup water.
Let stand for 5 minutes.
• In a medium saucepan, stir together cream and sugar
over medium-high heat. Cook until bubbles appear
around edge of pan and mixture is steaming. Remove
from heat. Add vanilla extract and gelatin mixture, stirring until well combined. Let mixture cool somewhat.
Transfer mixture to a liquid-measuring cup.
• Arrange 6 dessert dishes or glasses on a rimmed baking sheet. Divide cream mixture evenly among dishes.
Refrigerate until mixture is cold and firm, approximately
4 hours.
• Before serving, garnish with raspberries, blueberries,
blackberries, and mint sprigs, if desired.

*KITCHEN TIP: Before serving, toss fresh raspberries, blue-
berries, and blackberries in simple syrup, if desired. To make
simple syrup, stir together equal parts sugar and warm water
until sugar dissolves. Let cool before using.*

*MAKE-AHEAD TIP: Panna cottas can be made up to a day in
advance, covered, and refrigerated until ready to serve.*

Lacy Pecan Cookies
Makes 48

1 cup whole pecans
2 tablespoons unsalted butter, softened
1 cup firmly packed light brown sugar
1 large egg
1 teaspoon vanilla extract
¼ cup all-purpose flour
½ teaspoon baking powder
⅛ teaspoon salt
Garnish: dark chocolate melting wafers*, melted
    according to package instructions

• Preheat oven to 350°. Line several rimmed baking
sheets with parchment paper.
• Place pecans in the work bowl of a food processor,
and pulse until finely chopped. (Be careful not to over-
process.)
• In a large bowl, beat together butter and sugar with
mixer at high speed until light and fluffy. Add egg and
vanilla extract, beating until incorporated.
• In a small bowl, whisk together flour, baking powder,
and salt until combined. Add to butter mixture, beating
until incorporated. Stir in pecans.
• Using a levered 1-teaspoon scoop, drop batter 3 to 4
inches apart on prepared baking sheets. (Cookies will
spread as they bake.)
• Bake for 6 to 7 minutes, rotating pans halfway through.
Let cookies cool on baking sheets for 5 minutes. Using a
metal spatula, carefully transfer cookies to wire cooling
racks. Let cool completely.
• If desired, garnish cookies with a drizzle of melted
chocolate. Let chocolate set. Store cookies in an airtight
container with layers separated by wax paper for up to
3 days.

*We used Ghirardelli.

Cardamom-Orange Cakes with Browned Butter Frosting

Makes 10 servings

½ cup unsalted butter, softened
1 cup granulated sugar
2 large eggs
½ teaspoon vanilla extract
1½ cups cake flour
1 tablespoon fresh orange zest
1½ teaspoons baking powder
1 teaspoon ground cardamom
¼ teaspoon salt
½ cup whole milk
Browned Butter Frosting (recipe follows)
Garnish: orange curls*, fresh rosemary sprigs,
   and edible flowers**

• Preheat oven to 350°. Line a 15¼x10¼-inch rimmed baking sheet with parchment paper. Spray with cooking spray.
• In a large bowl, beat together butter and sugar with a mixer at medium-high speed until light and fluffy, approximately 3 minutes. Add eggs, one at a time, beating well after each addition. Add vanilla extract, beating until incorporated.
• In a medium bowl, whisk together flour, orange zest, baking powder, cardamom, and salt. Add flour mixture to butter mixture alternately with milk in thirds, beginning and ending with flour mixture, beating well after each addition. Using an offset spatula, spread mixture evenly into prepared pan. Tap pan on countertop several times to release air bubbles.
• Bake until edges of cake are golden brown and a wooden pick inserted in center comes out clean, 15 to 17 minutes. Let cool completely in pan. Using a sharp knife, cut cake in thirds lengthwise, and then cut in half widthwise.
• To assemble cakes, place a cake rectangle on a cutting board and spread Browned Butter Frosting in an even layer on cake rectangle. Top with another cake rectangle. Spread another even layer of frosting over cake layer. Top with another cake rectangle, creating a triple-stack cake. Spread another even layer of frosting over top cake rectangle. (Sides do not need to be frosted). Repeat with remaining cake rectangles and frosting to assemble another triple-stack cake. Freeze until firm, approximately 15 minutes.

• Using a serrated knife in a gentle sawing motion, trim and discard rough sides and ends of cakes so that whole cakes are even. Cut each cake into 5 (approximately 2¼x1¼-inch) rectangles.
• Garnish with orange curls, rosemary, and edible flowers, if desired. Serve immediately, or store in an airtight container and refrigerate for several hours. Let come to room temperature before serving.

*Using a channel knife or a zesting tool, cut long strips of orange peel. Wrap strips around a straw to shape. Using kitchen shears, cut curled peel to desired lengths. Use immediately.
**Edible flowers are available from Gourmet Sweet Botanicals, 800-931-7530, gourmetsweetbotanicals.com.

Salted Browned Butter Frosting

Makes 4½ cups

1½ cups unsalted butter, softened
5 cups confectioners' sugar
4 teaspoons vanilla extract
1 teaspoon fine sea salt*
2½ tablespoons whole milk
2 teaspoons heavy whipping cream

• In a medium saucepan, melt butter over medium-high heat until it foams. Using a rubber spatula, scrape bottom of pan to keep butter from burning so it will brown evenly. (Reduce heat, if necessary.) Let butter foam a second time. Stir, watching carefully so butter does not burn, until butter is a deep golden yellow and has a nutty aroma.
• Transfer browned butter to a heatproof bowl, and let cool to room temperature. Refrigerate until butter becomes solid but not hard.
• In a large bowl, beat chilled browned butter with a mixer at medium speed for 2 minutes. Add confectioners' sugar, beating at low speed until fluffy. Add vanilla extract and salt, beating to combine. Add milk and cream, beating at high speed until frosting is light and fluffy. Use immediately.

*Fine sea salt is important to use for the taste and texture of this frosting. Don't substitute another salt. If a sweeter, less salty frosting is desired, reduce amount of salt.

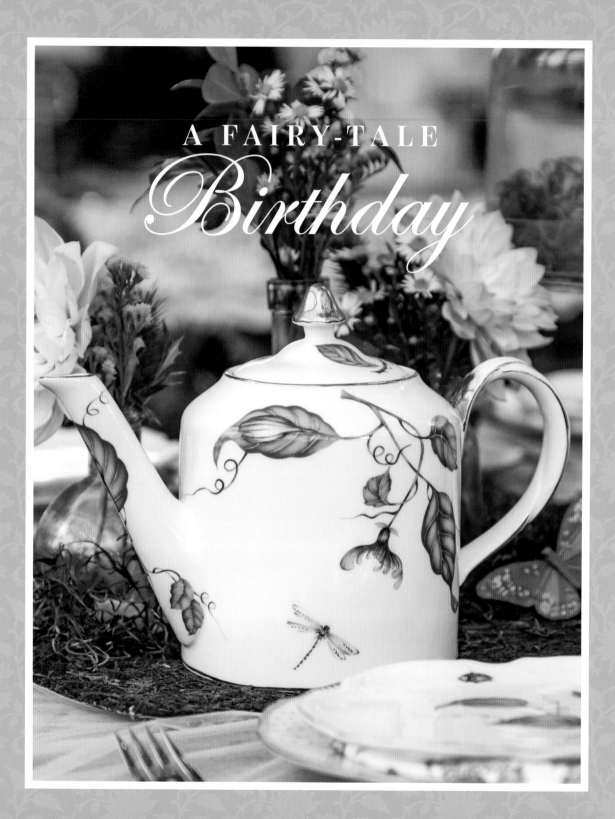

A FAIRY-TALE
Birthday

The
MENU

SCONE
Fairy Chocolate Scones

*Strawberry-Kiwi Caffeine-free
Fruit Infusion*

SAVORIES
BLT Swirls with
Tomato–Black Olive Ladybugs

Fairy Bites (Turkey &
Cream Cheese Tea Sandwiches
on Strawberry Bread)

Fruit Wands with
Honey-Lime Yogurt Dip

*Blueberry Caffeine-free
Fruit Infusion*

SWEETS
Fairy Pillows
(Honey-Orange Marshmallows)

Dragonflies & Butterflies
Sugar Cookies

Lemon Kiss Cake

*Banana Split Caffeine-free
Fruit Infusion*

Tea Pairings by Elmwood Inn Fine Teas
859-236-6641 • elmwoodinn.com

*Children will be delighted
to visit an enchanted
forest with the fairies for
an afternoon tea filled
with fanciful treats.*

Fairy Chocolate Scones
Makes approximately 18

2¾ cups all-purpose flour
⅓ cup granulated sugar
1 tablespoon baking powder
½ teaspoon baking soda
1 teaspoon salt
½ cup cold unsalted butter, cubed
½ cup white chocolate chips
½ cup semisweet chocolate chips
2 large eggs, lightly beaten
½ cup whole buttermilk
1 teaspoon vanilla extract

• Preheat oven to 425°. Line 2 rimmed baking sheets with parchment paper.
• In a large bowl, whisk together flour, sugar, baking powder, baking soda, and salt. Using a pastry blender or 2 forks, cut butter into flour mixture until it resembles coarse crumbs. Add white chocolate chips and semisweet chocolate chips, stirring to combine. Make a well in center of flour mixture.
• In a medium bowl, whisk together eggs, buttermilk, and vanilla extract. Add to flour mixture, stirring until a dough begins to form. Working gently, bring mixture together with hands until a dough forms. (If mixture seems dry and dough won't come together, add more buttermilk 1 tablespoon at a time.)
• Turn dough out onto a lightly floured surface, and knead gently until smooth by patting dough and folding it in half 4 to 5 times. Using a rolling pin, roll out dough to a 1-inch thickness. Using a 2-inch round cutter dipped in flour, cut as many scones as possible from dough, rerolling scraps as needed. Place scones 2 inches apart on prepared baking sheets.
• Bake until scones are golden brown, approximately 10 minutes.

BLT Swirls

Makes approximately 20 slices

12 slices bacon
½ cup mayonnaise
1 teaspoon fresh lemon juice
1 teaspoon seasoned salt*
4 burrito-size flour tortillas
4 cups chopped romaine lettuce
1 pint cherry tomatoes, washed and chopped
Garnish: Tomato–Black Olive Ladybugs
   (recipe follows)

• In a large skillet, cook bacon over medium heat until crisp, 4 to 6 minutes. Remove bacon, and let drain on paper towels. Using a sharp knife, chop bacon into fine pieces.
• In a small bowl, stir together mayonnaise, lemon juice, and seasoned salt. Spread a layer of mayonnaise mixture evenly onto each tortilla.
• On bottom half of each tortilla, sprinkle layers of lettuce, tomatoes, and bacon. Fold approximately 1 inch on sides of tortillas over filling. Beginning at bottom half, roll up each tortilla tightly, encasing filling. Wrap securely in plastic wrap, place seam side down, and refrigerate for up to 1 hour until ready to serve.
• Remove rolls from plastic wrap, and place on a cutting board. Using a sharp knife, cut each roll into 5 (1½-inch) slices.
• Garnish platter with Tomato–Black Olive Ladybugs, if desired. Serve immediately.

We used Lawry's Seasoned Salt.

Tomato–Black Olive Ladybugs

Makes 8

4 cherry tomatoes or grape tomatoes
4 medium pitted black olives
2 teaspoons mayonnaise

• Cut tomatoes in half lengthwise. Gently remove seeds from tomato halves. Cut each tomato half partially in half lengthwise, and gently separate cut so tomato half looks like wings but is still connected at one end.
• Cut olives in half horizontally.
• To assemble ladybugs in place on serving platter, trim each olive half to fit under the tomato wings for the ladybugs' abdomens. Rest a remaining half of olive on opposite end of tomato half for the ladybug's head, trimming olive slightly, if needed.
• Place mayonnaise in a small piping bag, and cut a very small opening in tip of piping bag. Pipe mayonnaise onto olive head of lady bug to resemble eyes and randomly onto tomato wings of ladybug to resemble polka dots. Serve immediately.

Fairy Bites (Turkey & Cream Cheese Tea Sandwiches on Strawberry Bread)

Makes 8

1 loaf Strawberry Bread (recipe follows)
4 ounces cream cheese, softened
8 ounces thinly sliced deli smoked turkey
Garnish: 2 small strawberries, hulled and quartered

• Using a serrated bread knife in a gentle sawing motion, cut bread into 8 slices. Trim and discard crusts from bread slices, and cut each bread slice into a 4x2-inch rectangle.
• Spread an even layer of cream cheese onto each bread slice. Top 4 bread slices evenly with turkey. Cover with remaining bread slices, cream cheese side down, to make 4 sandwiches.
• Using a serrated bread knife in a gentle sawing motion, cut sandwiches in half, creating 8 (2-inch) square tea sandwiches.
• Garnish each with a strawberry piece, if desired.

Strawberry Bread

Makes 1 (9-inch) loaf

1½ cups all-purpose flour
1 cup granulated sugar
½ teaspoon baking soda
½ teaspoon salt
¼ teaspoon pumpkin pie spice
¾ cup vegetable oil
2 large eggs, lightly beaten
1 (16-ounce) package frozen sliced strawberries,
   thawed and drained
Red gel food coloring (optional)

• Preheat oven to 350°. Spray a 9-inch loaf pan with nonstick baking spray.

- In a large bowl, whisk together flour, sugar, baking soda, salt, and pumpkin pie spice. Make a well in center of flour mixture.
- In a small bowl, stir together oil, eggs, strawberries, and desired amount of food coloring. Add to flour mixture, stirring just until moistened. Spoon batter into prepared loaf pan.

- Bake until a wooden pick inserted in center comes out clean, 60 to 75 minutes. Let cool in pan for 10 minutes. Remove from pan, and let cool completely on a wire rack. Place bread in an airtight container, and refrigerate for 1 hour or up to a day in advance before using for sandwiches.

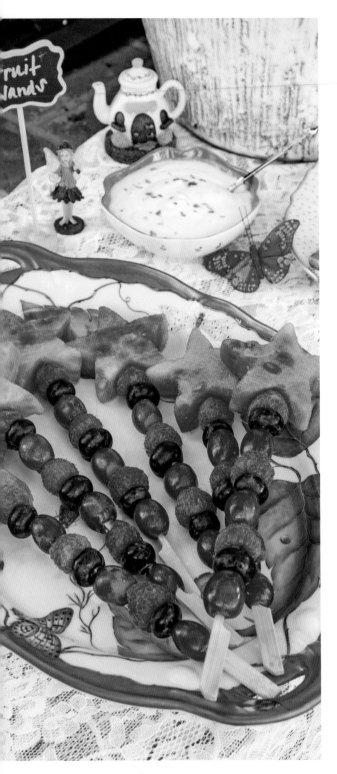

Fruit Wands with Honey-Lime Yogurt Dip
Makes 6

½ large seedless watermelon
18 large red grapes
1 pint blueberries
1 pint raspberries
6 large wooden skewers
Honey-Lime Yogurt Dip (recipe follows)

• Using a sharp knife, cut watermelon into 6 slices. Using a 4-inch star cutter, cut 6 stars from watermelon.
• Place a grape, a blueberry, and a raspberry onto a skewer, repeating pattern twice more. Using scissors, snip and discard pointed end from skewer. Cap skewer with a watermelon star. Repeat with remaining ingredients to make 6 wands.
• Serve immediately with Honey-Lime Yogurt Dip, or cover and refrigerate for up to an hour.

EDITOR'S NOTE: To prevent possible choking, children should be supervised when eating fruit such as blueberries, raspberries, and grapes.

Honey-Lime Yogurt Dip
Makes approximately 1 cup

1 cup whole milk yogurt
1 tablespoon honey
1 teaspoon fresh lime zest
1 tablespoon fresh lime juice

• In a small bowl, whisk together yogurt, honey, lime zest, and lime juice. Refrigerate until ready to serve.

Fairy wings and matching wands double as darling décor and party favors.

Fairy Pillows
(Honey-Orange Marshmallows)

Makes approximately 12

¼ cup confectioners' sugar
¼ cup cornstarch
3 (1-ounce) packages unflavored gelatin
1 cup ice water, divided
1½ cups granulated sugar
¾ cup light corn syrup
¼ cup honey
¼ teaspoon salt
½ teaspoon vanilla extract
½ teaspoon orange extract
Pink gel food coloring
Garnish: lime fruit slice candy

• In a small bowl, whisk together confectioners' sugar
and cornstarch. Sift mixture over a 9-inch square baking
pan. Shake pan gently to coat all sides. Gently tap pan to
remove excess sugar mixture, reserving for later.
• In the bowl of a stand mixer fitted with whisk attachment, stir together gelatin and ½ cup ice water; let stand
until softened, approximately 2 minutes.
• In a large saucepan, combine remaining ½ cup water,
granulated sugar, corn syrup, honey, and salt. Cook over
medium heat, stirring constantly, until sugar dissolves.
Cook, without stirring, until a candy thermometer registers 240°, 7 to 8 minutes. Remove from heat.
• With mixer running at low speed, slowly and carefully pour hot syrup over gelatin mixture against sides of
bowl. Increase speed to high, and beat until mixture is
thick and stiff peaks form, 11 to 14 minutes. Add vanilla
extract and orange extract, beating until incorporated,
approximately 1 minute. Add a few drops of pink food
coloring, folding into mixture to make streaks.
• Using an offset spatula sprayed with cooking spray,
immediately spread mixture into prepared pan, and
smooth top. Let dry for 8 to 12 hours.
• Sift reserved confectioners' sugar mixture onto a cutting board. Turn out marshmallow onto prepared board.
Using a 2-inch flower-shaped cutter dipped in reserved
confectioners' sugar mixture, cut 12 shapes from marshmallow. Store marshmallows at room temperature in an
airtight container with layers separated by wax paper for
up to 2 days.
• Garnish with lime fruit slice candy to resemble leaves,
if desired.

"May you touch dragonflies and stars, dance with fairies and talk to the moon. May you grow up with love and gracious hearts and people who care." —AUTHOR UNKNOWN

Dragonflies & Butterflies Sugar Cookies

Makes approximately 30

1 cup unsalted butter, softened
1¾ cups confectioners' sugar
1 large egg
1 teaspoon vanilla extract
3 cups all-purpose flour
1 teaspoon baking soda
1 teaspoon salt
1 teaspoon cream of tartar
Royal Icing (recipe follows)
Gel food coloring: yellow, purple, green, blue
Garnish: edible green pearlized powder

• In a large bowl, beat together butter and confectioners' sugar with a mixer at medium speed until light and fluffy, 2 to 3 minutes, stopping to scrape sides of bowl. Add egg and vanilla extract, beating until combined.
• In a medium bowl, whisk together flour, baking soda, salt, and cream of tartar. With mixer at low speed, gradually add flour mixture to butter mixture, beating together until a dough forms. Divide dough in half. Shape dough into discs, and wrap in plastic wrap. Refrigerate for at least 1 hour.
• Preheat oven to 350°. Line several baking sheets with parchment paper.
• On a lightly floured surface, roll half of dough to a ¼-inch thickness. (Lightly flour top of dough, if dough sticks to rolling pin.) Using a 5-inch butterfly-shaped cutter and a 4-inch dragonfly-shaped cutter dipped in flour, cut as many shapes as possible from dough, rerolling scraps as necessary. Using a small offset spatula, place cookies at least a ½ inch apart on prepared baking sheets. Repeat with remaining dough half.
• Bake until cookies are lightly browned, 7 to 10 minutes. Let cool for 1 minute on baking sheet. Remove cookies to a wire rack, and let cool completely.
• For butterfly cookies, in a medium bowl, stir together ¾ cup Royal Icing and a few drops yellow food coloring until well combined. Transfer icing to a resealable plastic bag, and snip off a corner of bag. Pipe around edges of butterfly cookies and fill in a concentric, circular motion, tapping cookies very gently on a flat surface to even icing.
• In a small bowl, stir together ¼ cup Royal icing and a few drops purple food coloring until well combined. Transfer icing to a resealable plastic bag, and snip off a corner of bag. Pipe a dot onto yellow icing at each corner of butterfly wings. Gently pull a wooden pick through purple icing to swirl. Let dry for 30 minutes.
• Pipe remaining yellow icing onto butterfly bodies. Let dry for at least 4 hours.
• For dragonfly cookies, in a medium bowl, stir together remaining 1 cup Royal Icing and a few drops blue and green food coloring to achieve a pleasing color. Transfer icing to a resealable plastic bag, and snip off a corner of bag. Pipe around edges of dragonfly cookies and fill in a concentric motion, tapping cookies very gently on a flat surface to even icing. Let dry for 30 minutes.
• Brush dragonfly wings with green pearlized powder, if desired. Pipe remaining blue-green icing onto dragonfly bodies. Let dry for at least 4 hours.

MAKE-AHEAD TIP: Undecorated cookies can be placed in an airtight container with layers separated by wax paper and frozen for up to a month. Thaw before decorating. Store decorated cookies at room temperature in an airtight container with layers separated by wax paper for up to 3 days.

Royal Icing

Makes 2 cups

4 cups confectioners' sugar
¼ cup meringue powder
½ cup warm water

• In a large bowl, whisk together confectioners' sugar and meringue powder until combined. Gradually add warm water, whisking together until smooth. Use immediately.

Lemon Kiss Cake

Makes 1 (8-inch) cake, approximately 12 servings

1 cup unsalted butter, softened
1⅔ cup granulated sugar
3 large eggs
1 teaspoon vanilla extract
1 teaspoon lemon extract
2⅓ cups cake flour
1½ teaspoons baking powder
½ teaspoon salt
¼ teaspoon baking soda
¾ cup whole buttermilk
2 tablespoons fresh lemon juice
Lemon-Buttermilk Frosting (recipe follows)
Gel food coloring: green, pink

• Preheat oven to 350°. Spray 3 (8-inch) round cake pans with baking spray with flour.
• In a large bowl, beat together butter and sugar with a mixer at medium speed until light and fluffy, 3 to 4 minutes, stopping occasionally to scrape down sides of bowl. Add eggs, one at a time, beating well after each addition. Add vanilla extract and lemon extract, stirring until incorporated.

• In a medium bowl, whisk together flour, baking powder, salt, and baking soda. Gradually add flour mixture to butter mixture alternately with buttermilk, beginning and ending with flour mixture, beating just until combined after each addition. Add lemon juice, beating well.
• Divide batter among prepared pans. Using an offset spatula, smooth tops, if necessary.
• Bake until a wooden pick inserted in centers of cake layers comes out clean, 16 to 19 minutes. Let cool in pans for 10 minutes. Remove from pans, and let cool completely on wire racks.
• Using an offset spatula, spread approximately 3½ cups Lemon-Buttermilk Frosting between layers and on top and sides of cake.
• In a medium bowl, stir together 1¼ cups Lemon-Buttermilk Frosting and a few drops green food coloring until well combined. (Add more food coloring to achieve desired color.) Place frosting in a piping bag fitted with a medium star tip (Wilton #30). Pipe green stars on tops and sides of cake, as desired.
• In a small bowl, stir together remaining ¼ cups Lemon-Buttermilk Frosting and a few drops pink food coloring until well combined. (Add more food coloring to achieve desired color.) Place frosting in a piping bag fitted with a smaller star tip (Wilton #21). Pipe pink stars randomly on top and around sides of cake, as desired.

Lemon-Buttermilk Frosting

Makes approximately 5 cups

2 cups unsalted butter, softened
1 (32-ounce) bag confectioners' sugar
2 tablespoons fresh lemon juice
1½ teaspoons lemon extract
1 teaspoon vanilla extract
½ cups whole buttermilk

• In a large bowl, beat butter with a mixer at medium speed until light and creamy. Add 1 cup confectioners' sugar, beating at low speed until combined. Increase mixer to medium speed, beating well. Repeat with remaining confectioners' sugar, scraping sides of bowl as needed.
• Add lemon juice, lemon extract, and vanilla extract to butter mixture, beating at medium-high speed until combined. Gradually add buttermilk, beating at medium-high speed until frosting is desired consistency. (Frosting should be spreadable, but not runny.)

Fairy Bites and BLT Swirls

Lemon Kiss Cake

SWEET

Celebration

The
MENU

SCONE

Orange, Ricotta & Poppy Seed
Scones

Brontë Sisters' Black Tea Blend

SAVORIES

Ham and Havarti Tea Sandwiches

Mustardy Egg Salad
Tea Sandwiches

Smoked Salmon and Cucumber
Tea Sandwiches

Edith Wharton's Black Tea Blend

SWEETS

Blueberry-Lemon
Mini Phyllo Tartlets

Carrot Cake Rooibos
Shortbread Cookies

Strawberry-Lavender Cakes

*Emily Dickinson's
Jasmine Tea Blend*

Tea Pairings by Simpson & Vail
800-282-8327 • svtea.com

*Beautiful blooms and
pretty china set the tone
for a happy birthday
celebration featuring
dainty teatime nibbles.*

Orange, Ricotta & Poppy Seed Scones

Makes 12

2½ cups all-purpose flour
⅓ cup granulated sugar
2 tablespoons fresh orange zest
1 tablespoon poppy seeds
1 tablespoon baking powder
½ teaspoon salt
4 tablespoons cold unsalted butter, cubed
½ cup whole-milk ricotta cheese
½ cup cold heavy whipping cream, divided
½ teaspoon vanilla extract

• Preheat oven to 375°. Line a rimmed baking sheet with parchment paper.
• In a large bowl, whisk together flour, sugar, orange zest, poppy seeds, baking powder, and salt. Using a pastry blender or 2 forks, cut butter into flour mixture until it resembles coarse crumbs.
• In a small bowl, stir together ricotta cheese, ¼ cup plus 3 tablespoons cold cream, and vanilla extract until combined. Add cheese mixture to flour mixture, stirring until a dough begins to form. Working gently, bring mixture together with hands until a dough forms. (If mixture seems dry and dough won't come together, add more cream, 1 tablespoon at a time.)
• Turn out dough onto a lightly floured surface, and knead gently until smooth by patting dough and folding it in half 3 to 4 times. Using a rolling pin, roll out dough to a 1-inch thickness. Using a 2-inch round cutter dipped in flour, cut 12 scones from dough, rerolling scraps as necessary. Place scones 2 inches apart on prepared baking sheet.
• Brush tops of scones with remaining 1 tablespoon cream.
• Bake until edges of scones are golden brown and a wooden pick inserted in centers comes out clean, 17 to 19 minutes. Serve warm.

RECOMMENDED CONDIMENTS:
Devonshire Cream
Orange Marmalade

Ham and Havarti Tea Sandwiches

Makes 12

8 large slices potato bread
2 tablespoons mayonnaise
2 tablespoons spicy brown mustard
6 deli slices Havarti cheese
12 deli slices honey ham

• Using a serrated bread knife in a gentle sawing motion, trim and discard crusts from bread to make 8 (4½x3-inch) rectangles. Stack 2 bread slices. Cut 3 (3x1½-inch) rectangles from bread stack. Repeat with remaining bread slices. (You should have 24 bread rectangles.)
• In a small bowl, stir together mayonnaise and mustard until combined to make an aïoli. Spread a layer of aïoli onto all bread rectangles.
• Using a sharp knife, cut 12 (3x1½-inch) cheese rectangles.
• On aioli side of 12 bread rectangles, place on each 1 cheese rectangle and 1 ham slice, folding ham back and forth upon itself to fit width of bread. Cover each with a remaining bread rectangle, aïoli side down. Using kitchen scissors, trim excess ham from ends of sandwich, if desired. Serve immediately, or cover with damp paper towels, place in covered container, and refrigerate for a few hours before serving.

Mustardy Egg Salad Tea Sandwiches

Makes 12

8 large hard-cooked eggs, peeled and chopped*
¼ cup mayonnaise
1 tablespoon yellow mustard
1 tablespoon Dijon mustard
1 tablespoon Creole mustard
1 tablespoon finely chopped fresh chives
¼ teaspoon salt
⅛ teaspoon ground black pepper
8 large slices honey wheat bread

• In a large bowl, stir together eggs, mayonnaise, yellow mustard, Dijon mustard, Creole mustard, chives, salt, and pepper until combined. Spread a thick even layer of egg salad onto 4 bread slices. Cover with remaining bread slices to make 4 whole sandwiches.
• Using a serrated bread knife in a gentle sawing motion, trim and discard crusts from sandwiches to make

4½x3-inch rectangles. Cut each sandwich into 3 (3x 1½-inch) finger sandwiches. Serve immediately, or cover with damp paper towels, place in a covered container, and refrigerate for a few hours before serving.

For instructions on how to hard-cook eggs, please see the first step of Dinosaur Eggs Tea Sandwiches on page 105.

Smoked Salmon and Cucumber Tea Sandwiches

Makes 12

8 large slices white sandwich bread
Lemon–Crème Fraîche Spread (recipe follows)
12 deli slices smoked salmon
½ cup loosely packed baby arugula
24 thin slices English cucumber

• Using a serrated bread knife in a gentle sawing motion, trim and discard crusts from bread to make 8 (4½x3-inch) rectangles. Stack 2 bread slices. Cut 3 (3x1½-inch) rectangles from bread stack. Repeat with remaining bread slices. (You should have 24 bread rectangles.)
• Spread a layer of Lemon–Crème Fraîche Spread onto all bread rectangles. Trim salmon slices to fit bread rectangles. On spread side of 12 bread rectangles, place on each a few arugula leaves, 1 salmon slice, and 2 cucumber slices. Cover each with a remaining bread rectangle, spread side down. Serve immediately, or cover with damp paper towels, place in a covered container, and refrigerate for a few hours before serving.

Lemon–Crème Fraîche Spread

Makes ½ cup

½ cup crème fraîche
1 tablespoon mayonnaise
1 teaspoon fresh lemon zest
½ teaspoon fresh lemon juice
⅛ teaspoon ground black pepper

• In a small bowl, stir together crème fraîche, mayonnaise, lemon zest, lemon juice, and pepper until combined. Store in a covered container and refrigerate until ready to use.

MAKE-AHEAD TIP: *Lemon–Crème Fraîche Spread can be made a day in advance for flavors to meld.*

Blueberry-Lemon Mini Phyllo Tartlets

Makes 15

1 (8-ounce) container mascarpone cheese
3 tablespoons confectioners' sugar
1 tablespoon heavy whipping cream
¼ teaspoon vanilla extract
⅓ cup prepared lemon curd
1 (1.9-ounce) box frozen graham cracker flavor
    phyllo shells*, thawed and crispened according
    to package directions
15 blueberries
Garnish: 15 mint sprigs

• In a medium bowl, beat together mascarpone cheese, confectioners' sugar, cream, and vanilla extract with a mixer at medium speed until combined. Transfer mascarpone mixture to a piping bag fitted with a large open star tip (Wilton #1M).
• Place lemon curd in another piping bag fitted with a medium round tip (Wilton #12).
• Pipe a thin layer of lemon curd into bottoms of phyllo shells. Pipe an upright frill of mascarpone mixture on top of lemon curd layer. Using point of little finger, make a small depression in center of mascarpone mixture. Pipe a small button of lemon curd into depression. Place a blueberry on top of lemon curd.
• Garnish each tartlet with a fresh mint sprig, if desired. Serve immediately, or refrigerate for up to 1 hour before serving.

We used Athens Graham Cracker Flavor Phyllo Shells.

Carrot Cake Rooibos Shortbread Cookies

Makes 24

1 cup all-purpose flour
1 tablespoon carrot cake–flavored rooibos loose tea*
¼ teaspoon salt
½ cup unsalted butter, softened
¼ cup confectioners' sugar
½ teaspoon vanilla extract

• In a medium bowl, whisk together flour, loose tea, and salt until combined.
• In a large bowl, beat together butter, confectioners' sugar, and vanilla extract with a mixer at high speed until light and creamy. Add flour mixture, beating until incorporated. Shape dough into a disk, and wrap

securely in plastic wrap. Refrigerate until dough is hard but still soft enough to roll out, approximately 1 hour.
• Preheat oven to 350°. Line 2 rimmed baking sheets with parchment paper.
• Place dough between 2 sheets of wax paper. Using a rolling pin, roll out dough to a ¼-inch thickness. Place dough with wax paper onto another rimmed baking sheet. Freeze for 15 minutes.
• Using a 1¾-inch fluted square cutter dipped in flour, cut 24 shapes from dough, rerolling scraps as necessary. (Refrigerate dough scraps again before rerolling.) Place cookies 2 inches apart on prepared baking sheets.
• Bake until cookies are set and edges are light golden brown, 10 to 12 minutes. Transfer cookies to a wire cooling rack and let cool completely. Store cookies in an airtight container until ready to serve.

We used Simpson & Vail's Carrot Cake Cupcake Green Rooibos Tisane, 800-282-8327, svtea.com.

Strawberry-Lavender Cakes

Makes 16

⅓ cup whole milk
1 teaspoon distilled white vinegar
2 cups cake flour
1 teaspoon baking powder
1 teaspoon dried culinary lavender
½ teaspoon salt
¼ teaspoon baking soda
½ cup unsalted butter, softened
1¼ cups granulated sugar
½ cup seedless strawberry jam
3 large eggs
½ teaspoon vanilla extract
Red liquid food coloring
Strawberry Buttercream (recipe follows)
Garnish: fresh lavender buds*

• Preheat oven to 350°. Line a 17¼x11½-inch rimmed baking sheet with parchment paper and spray with cooking spray.
• In a small bowl, stir together milk and vinegar until combined. Let stand for 10 minutes for milk to clabber.
• In a medium bowl, whisk together flour, baking powder, dried lavender, salt, and baking soda until combined.
• In a large bowl, beat together butter and sugar with a mixer at high speed until light and fluffy, approximately 3 minutes. Add jam and eggs, one at a time, beating well after each addition. Add vanilla extract and food coloring

to achieve desired color, beating to combine. Add flour mixture to butter mixture, alternately with milk mixture, beginning and ending with flour mixture, beating well after each addition. Pour batter into prepared baking sheet. Using an offset spatula, spread batter evenly in baking sheet. Tap baking sheet several times on countertop to reduce air bubbles in batter.

• Bake until a wooden pick inserted near center comes out clean, 14 to 16 minutes. Let cool completely in baking sheet. Freeze for 1 hour.

• Using a 2-inch round cutter, cut 32 circles from frozen cake, discarding scraps. Let cake rounds thaw completely.

• Place Strawberry Buttercream in a piping bag fitted with a large open star tip (Wilton #1M). Pipe buttercream onto 16 cake rounds. Top each with a plain cake round, and pipe buttercream decoratively onto top of each cake round. Serve immediately, or place in a covered container and refrigerate for a few hours. Let come to room temperature before serving.

• Garnish with lavender buds, if desired.

Edible fresh lavender is available from Gourmet Sweet Botanicals, 800-931-7530, gourmetsweetbotanicals.com.

Strawberry Buttercream
Makes 3 cups

1 cup unsalted butter, softened
5 cups confectioners' sugar
2 tablespoons whole milk
2 teaspoons strawberry extract
½ teaspoon salt
Red liquid food coloring

• In a large bowl, beat together butter, confectioners' sugar, milk, strawberry extract, salt, and desired amount of food coloring with a mixer, starting at low speed and gradually increasing to high, until combined and fluffy. Use immediately.

TEA-REX

Birthday

The
MENU

SCONE
Tea-rrific Blueberry Scones
African Autumn Herbal Tea

SAVORIES
Dinosaur Egg Sandwiches
Carnivore Cups
Honey-Lime Pterodactyl Wings
Indigo Punch

SWEETS
Dinosaur Eye Cookies
Peanut Butter Fossil Fudge
Dino-mite Cookies and Cream
Birthday Cakes
Mango Fruit Tea

Tea Pairings by Harney & Sons
800-832-8463 • harney.com

The birthday boy and his guests are sure to enjoy an afternoon tea full of prehistoric-themed foods like Honey-Lime Pterodactyl Wings and Peanut Butter Fossil Fudge.

Tea-rrific Blueberry Scones
Makes 12

2¾ cups all-purpose flour
⅓ cup granulated sugar
1 tablespoon baking powder
1 teaspoon salt
6 tablespoons cold unsalted butter, cubed
½ cup sour cream, divided
1 cup whole milk
½ teaspoon vanilla extract
½ cup small blueberries
½ cup confectioners' sugar

• Preheat oven to 350°. Line a baking sheet with parchment paper.
• In a large bowl, whisk together flour, sugar, baking powder, and salt. Using a pastry blender or 2 forks, cut butter into flour mixture until it resembles coarse crumbs.
• In a medium bowl, whisk together ¼ cup sour cream, milk, and vanilla extract. Add to flour mixture, stirring until a dough begins to form. Add blueberries, stirring gently to incorporate. Working very gently, bring mixture together with hands until a dough forms.
• Turn out dough out onto a lightly floured surface, and knead gently until smooth by patting dough and folding it in half 6 to 7 times. Divide dough into 2 equal pieces. Shape each piece into 1-inch-thick disks. Using a sharp knife, cut each disk into 6 wedges. Place wedges 2 inches apart on prepared baking sheet.
• Bake until edges of scones are lightly golden, 15 to 20 minutes. Cool on baking sheet for 5 minutes. Transfer scones to wire racks. Let cool completely.
• In a small bowl, whisk together confectioners' sugar and remaining ¼ cup sour cream until smooth. Drizzle over cooled scones. Serve immediately.

Partygoers will be entertained looking for the hidden—and not so hidden—dinosaurs, robots, and monsters in the appropriately named Calamityware dishes.

Dinosaur Egg Sandwiches

Makes 10

10 large eggs
½ cup mayonnaise
½ cup chopped bread and butter pickles
¼ teaspoon seasoned salt
10 slices pumpernickel rye swirl bread, frozen

• In a large saucepan, place eggs in a single layer; add water to a depth of 3 inches. Bring to a boil over medium-high heat. Cover, remove from heat, and let stand for 15 minutes. Drain immediately. Fill saucepan with cold water and ice. Let stand until cool. Tap eggs firmly on counter until cracks form all over shell. Peel under cold running water. Using a sharp knife, finely chop eggs.
• In a medium bowl, stir together eggs, mayonnaise, pickles, and seasoned salt until combined.
• Using a 3- to 3½-inch egg-shaped cutter, cut 2 shapes from each frozen bread slice, discarding scraps.
• Spread a layer of egg salad onto 10 bread pieces. Cover each with a remaining bread piece. Serve immediately, or lightly cover with damp paper towels, place in a covered container, and refrigerate for up to 1 hour.

Carnivore Cups

Makes 10

1 (8.5-ounce) box corn muffin mix*
1 large egg, lightly beaten
⅓ cup whole milk
1 cup shredded extra-sharp Cheddar cheese
6 slices cooked bacon, chopped
½ cup diced ham

• Preheat oven to 400°. Line 10 wells of a 12-well muffin pan with paper cupcake liners.
• In a large bowl, whisk together muffin mix, egg, and milk. Add cheese, bacon, and ham to muffin mix, stirring until incorporated. Divide muffin mix among prepared cups.
• Bake until muffins are lightly golden and a wooden pick inserted in centers comes out clean, approximately 12 to 15 minutes. Let cool in pan for 5 minutes. Serve warm.

*We used Jiffy.

EDITOR'S NOTE: *Choose a variety of raw vegetables and fruit to serve as "Herbivore Bites" along with the savory recipes in this menu.*

Honey-Lime Pterodactyl Wings

Makes 12

12 bone-in chicken wings (approximately 3 pounds)
2 tablespoons vegetable oil
½ teaspoon salt
½ teaspoon freshly ground black pepper
½ cup honey
1 tablespoon fresh lime zest
⅓ cup fresh lime juice (2 to 3 large limes)
2 teaspoons garlic salt

• Preheat oven to 400°. Line a rimmed baking sheet with foil.
• Arrange chicken wings in a single layer on prepared baking sheet. Drizzle with oil, tossing gently to coat. Sprinkle wings with salt and pepper.
• Bake until wings are lightly golden on edges, 15 to 20 minutes. Remove from oven.
• In a small saucepan, whisk together honey, lime zest, lime juice, and garlic salt. Cook over medium-low heat until mixture is hot and smooth, whisking often, 5 to 7 minutes. Remove from heat.
• Increase oven temperature to 450°.
• Brush chicken wings with honey-lime mixture.
• Bake until wings are golden brown, and an instant-read thermometer inserted in thickest part of chicken registers 165°, approximately 4 minutes. Let cool 5 to 10 minutes before serving.

Dinosaur Eye Cookies

Makes approximately 30

½ cup unsalted butter, softened
¾ cup granulated sugar
1 large egg yolk, room temperature
2 teaspoons fresh lemon zest
2 teaspoons fresh lemon juice
½ teaspoon vanilla extract
1⅔ cups all-purpose flour
¼ teaspoon salt
⅓ cup orange marmalade

• Line 2 baking sheets with parchment paper.
• In a large bowl, beat together butter and sugar with a mixer at medium speed until light and fluffy, 2 to 3 minutes, stopping to scrape sides of bowl as needed. Add egg yolk, beating until combined. Add lemon zest, lemon juice, and vanilla extract, beating until well combined.
• In a medium bowl, whisk together flour and salt. Add flour mixture to butter mixture all at once, beating at low speed just until combined. Cover and refrigerate dough just until firm, approximately 1 hour.
• Preheat oven to 350°.
• Let dough stand at room temperature for 5 minutes. Divide dough into 30 equal portions, and roll into 1-inch balls. Place each ball on prepared baking sheets. Using a damp finger, gently press in center of ball to make an indentation. Fill each indentation with approximately ½ teaspoon orange marmalade.
• Bake until cookies are lightly golden, 16 to 19 minutes. Let cool for 5 minutes on baking sheet. Transfer cookies to wire racks, and let cool completely.

Peanut Butter Fossil Fudge

Makes approximately 12 pieces

2 cups granulated sugar
½ cup evaporated milk
1½ cups peanut butter
1 (7-oz) jar marshmallow crème
¼ teaspoon vanilla extract
¼ teaspoon salt
Food-safe dinosaur toy

• Line an 8-inch square baking pan with foil. Spray with cooking spray.
• In a large nonstick saucepan, stir together sugar and evaporated milk. Bring to a boil over medium heat, stirring often. Boil for another 3 minutes without stirring. Remove saucepan from heat.
• Add peanut butter, stirring until combined. Add marshmallow crème, stirring until smooth. Add vanilla extract and salt, stirring well.
• Spoon into prepared pan. Press top of fudge gently with parchment paper to smooth. Let fudge set for 15 minutes.
• Using a food-safe dinosaur toy, gently press dinosaur feet into fudge, if desired. Let fudge cool completely until set, approximately 4 hours.
• Using a sharp knife, cut fudge into 12 pieces. Store fudge in an airtight container at room temperature.

Dino-mite Cookies and Cream Birthday Cake

Makes 1 (9-inch), 14 to 16 servings

2½ cups whole milk
1 cup unsalted butter
4 ounces bittersweet chocolate, chopped
4 ounces semisweet chocolate, chopped
2⅔ cups all-purpose flour
2 cups granulated sugar
⅓ cup unsweetened cocoa powder
1 teaspoon baking soda
½ teaspoon salt
3 large eggs
1 teaspoon vanilla extract
Vanilla Buttercream (recipe follows)
1 cup crushed chocolate wafer cookies
Garnish: crushed chocolate cookie wafers,
    chocolate rocks, and food-safe toy dinosaur

• Preheat oven to 325°. Spray 3 (9-inch) round baking pans with cooking spray. Line pans with parchment rounds.
• In a large saucepan, combine milk, butter, bittersweet chocolate, and semisweet chocolate. Cook over medium-low heat until butter and chocolate melt, whisking often, 4 to 6 minutes. Remove mixture from heat and let cool for 15 minutes.
• In a large bowl, whisk together flour, sugar, cocoa powder, baking soda, and salt.
• In a separate large bowl, beat together eggs and vanilla extract with a mixer at medium-low speed. Add cooled chocolate mixture alternately with flour mixture to egg mixture, beginning and ending with chocolate mixture, beating just until combined after each addition. Divide batter evenly among prepared pans.
• Bake until a wooden pick inserted in centers of cake layers comes out clean, 25 to 28 minutes. Let cool in pans for 5 minutes. Transfer cakes to wire racks, and let cool completely.
• In a medium bowl, stir together 2½ cups Vanilla Buttercream and crushed cookies. Using an offset spatula, spread half of buttercream mixture onto 1 cake layer. Top with a second cake layer, and spread with remaining buttercream mixture. Top with remaining cake layer.
• Using an offset spatula, spread remaining 3½ cups Vanilla Buttercream on sides and top of cake.
• Garnish with crushed cookies, chocolate rocks, and dinosaur, if desired.

Vanilla Buttercream

Makes approximately 6 cups

2 cups unsalted butter, softened
10 cups confectioners' sugar
¼ cup heavy whipping cream
1 teaspoon vanilla extract

• In a large bowl, beat butter with a mixer at medium speed until light and creamy, approximately 3 minutes. Add confectioners' sugar, 1 cup at a time, beating at low speed after each addition until combined. Add cream and vanilla extract, beating at medium-high speed until light and fluffy. Use immediately.

GENTLEMANLY
Birthday

The
MENU

SCONE
Cheddar-Pimiento Scones

Hu-Kwa Tea

SAVORIES
Smoked Whitefish Tea Sandwiches

Buffalo Chicken & Slaw
Tea Sandwiches

Bacon-Jalapeño Deviled Eggs

*Organic Yunnan Golden Buds
Black Tea*

SWEETS
Apple-Blackberry Tartlets

Spiced Raisin-Walnut Bars

Chocolate Cake with
Peanut Butter Mousse

Brandy Oolong Tea

Tea Pairings by Mark T. Wendell Tea Company
978-635-9200 • marktwendell.com

*Honor the special man in
your life with a hearty tea
menu served buffet-style
to friends and family in a
refined, yet relaxed setting*

Cheddar-Pimiento Scones
Makes 8

2½ cups all-purpose flour
1 tablespoon granulated sugar
1 tablespoon baking powder
½ teaspoon salt
⅛ teaspoon ground black pepper
⅛ teaspoon ground chipotle pepper
4 tablespoons cold unsalted butter, cubed
1¼ cups coarsely shredded extra-sharp
   Cheddar cheese
¼ cup freshly grated Parmesan cheese
3 tablespoons diced pimientos, well drained
½ cup plus 1 tablespoon cold heavy whipping cream,
   divided
2 large eggs, divided
¼ teaspoon hot sauce*

• Preheat oven to 375°. Line a rimmed baking sheet with parchment paper.
• In a large bowl, whisk together flour, sugar, baking powder, salt, black pepper, and chipotle pepper. Using a pastry blender or 2 forks, cut in butter until mixture resembles coarse crumbs. Add Cheddar cheese, Parmesan cheese, and pimientos, stirring well.
• In a small bowl, whisk together ½ cup cream, 1 egg, and hot sauce. Add to flour mixture, stirring until a dough begins to form. Working gently, bring mixture together with hands until a dough forms. (If mixture seems dry and dough won't come together, add more cream, 1 tablespoon at a time.)
• Turn dough out onto a lightly floured surface, and knead gently until smooth by patting dough and folding it in half 4 to 5 times. Using a rolling pin, roll out dough to a 1-inch thickness. Using a floured 2¼-inch fluted round cutter dipped in flour, cut 8 scones from dough. Place scones 2 inches apart on prepared baking sheet.
• In a small bowl, whisk together remaining 1 tablespoon cream and remaining egg. Brush tops of scones with egg mixture.
• Bake until edges of scones are golden brown and a wooden pick inserted in centers comes out clean, 18 to 20 minutes. Serve warm.

We used Tabasco.

RECOMMENDED CONDIMENTS:
Softened Butter
Red Pepper Jelly

Smoked Whitefish Tea Sandwiches

Makes 12

¾ pound smoked whitefish*, skin and bones removed
¼ cup mayonnaise
3 tablespoons sour cream
2 tablespoons chopped fresh chives
1 tablespoon chopped fresh parsley
2 teaspoons fresh lemon juice
¼ teaspoon salt
¼ teaspoon ground black pepper
¼ teaspoon ground white pepper
8 large slices multi-seed bread

• In a medium bowl and using a fork, flake fish into pieces. Stir in mayonnaise, sour cream, chives, parsley, lemon juice, salt, black pepper, and white pepper until well combined. Cover and refrigerate until cold, approximately 4 hours and up to a day.
• Spread a thick even layer of whitefish mixture onto 4 bread slices. Cover with remaining bread slices. Using a serrated bread knife in a gentle sawing motion, trim and discard crusts from sandwiches. Cut each sandwich into 3 equal rectangular sandwiches. Serve immediately, or cover with damp paper towels, place in a covered container, and refrigerate for a few hours until serving time.

We used Blue Hill Bay.

Buffalo Chicken & Slaw Tea Sandwiches

Makes 16

⅓ cup mayonnaise
1 tablespoon blue cheese crumbles
½ teaspoon hot sauce*
⅛ teaspoon ground black pepper
8 large slices potato bread*
8 large slices deli-style buffalo chicken*
Classic Coleslaw (recipe follows), well drained

• In a small bowl, stir together mayonnaise, blue cheese, hot sauce, and pepper to make an aïoli. Use aïoli immediately, or cover and refrigerate for up to a day.
• Spread a layer of aïoli onto bread slices. On aïoli side of 4 bread slices, arrange chicken in a ruffled fashion, and top with a layer of Classic Coleslaw. Cover with remaining bread slices, aïoli side down.
• Using a serrated bread knife in a gentle sawing motion, trim and discard crusts from each sandwich to make a 3-inch square. Cut each sandwich diagonally into 4 triangles. Serve immediately, or cover with damp paper towels, place in a covered container, and refrigerate for a few hours until serving time.

We used Tabasco, Pepperidge Farm Farmhouse Style, and Boar's Head.

Classic Coleslaw

Makes 3 cups

3 cups very finely chopped cabbage
¼ cup mayonnaise
1 tablespoon granulated sugar
1 tablespoon apple cider vinegar
¼ teaspoon salt
⅛ teaspoon ground black pepper

• In a medium bowl, stir together cabbage, mayonnaise, sugar, vinegar, salt, and pepper until well combined. Place in covered container and refrigerate until very cold, up to a day. Stir and drain well before using.

Bacon-Jalapeño Deviled Eggs

Makes 12

6 large eggs, hard-cooked and peeled
⅓ cup mayonnaise
1 tablespoon Creole mustard
2 teaspoons yellow mustard
⅛ teaspoon salt
⅛ teaspoon ground black pepper
⅛ teaspoon ground white pepper
1 tablespoon minced very mild jalapeño peppers*
Garnish: 12 squares cooked bacon and 12 slices
    very mild jalapeño peppers*

• Cut eggs in half lengthwise. Remove yolks, and set whites aside.
• In a medium bowl and using a fork, mash yolks finely.

Stir in mayonnaise, Creole mustard, yellow mustard, salt, black pepper, and white pepper until well combined. Stir in minced jalapeño peppers. Transfer mixture to a piping bag fitted with a large open star tip (Wilton # 829). Pipe mixture into egg white halves. Refrigerate until cold, approximately 1 hour.
• Just before serving, garnish each egg half with a cooked bacon square and a jalapeño slice, if desired.

We used Mezzetta Deli-Sliced Tamed Jalapeño Peppers.

MAKE-AHEAD TIP: *Eggs can be prepared a day in advance. Store egg white halves in a covered container in the refrigerator. Blot on paper towels before using. Yolk mixture can be prepared a day in advance and stored in a separate container in the refrigerator. Pipe into whites just before serving.*

Apple-Blackberry Tartlets

Makes 8

1 (14.1-ounce) package refrigerated piecrust dough
(2 sheets)
2 tablespoons unsalted butter
1 cup diced, peeled Fuji apple
1 cup diced, peeled Golden Delicious apple
⅓ cup apple juice
1 teaspoon fresh lemon juice
2 tablespoons granulated sugar
2 tablespoons firmly packed dark brown sugar
½ teaspoon ground cinnamon
½ cup blackberries, cut in half
⅓ cup unsweetened applesauce
¼ teaspoon vanilla extract
1 cup honey-hemp granola*
Vanilla ice cream (optional)

• Preheat oven to 450°.
• On a lightly floured surface, unroll piecrust dough. Referring to page 133, using a 4-inch round cutter, cut 8 rounds from dough. Press rounds into 8 (3½-inch) tartlet pans, trimming edges as necessary. Using a fork, prick bottom of dough in each tartlet pan several times. Place tartlet pans on a rimmed baking sheet. Freeze for 15 minutes.
• Bake until light golden brown, approximately 7 to 9 minutes. Let cool completely before carefully removing shells from pans.
• In a medium sauté pan, melt butter over medium-high heat. Add apples, apple juice, lemon juice, granulated sugar, brown sugar, and cinnamon, stirring to combine. Cook, covered, for approximately 10 minutes, stirring occasionally. (Apples should feel tender when pierced with tip of knife) Uncover, add blackberries, and continue to cook until liquid has reduced and is somewhat syrupy, 3 to 5 minutes. Remove from heat, and add applesauce and vanilla extract, stirring to combine. Let mixture cool to room temperature.
• Just before serving, fill tartlet shells with fruit mixture and sprinkle with granola. Serve with vanilla ice cream, if desired.

We used Farmers We Know Sprouted Honey Hemp Granola.

MAKE-AHEAD TIP: Tartlet shells can be made earlier in the day and stored in an airtight container. Apple mixture can be made a day in advance, placed in a covered container, and refrigerated. Let come to room temperature before using.

Spiced Raisin-Walnut Bars

Makes 12

½ cup golden raisins
4 tablespoons unsalted butter, softened
⅓ cup granulated sugar
⅓ firmly packed light brown sugar
1 large egg
1 teaspoon vanilla extract
1 cup all-purpose flour
1 teaspoon baking powder
½ teaspoon ground allspice
¼ teaspoon salt
¼ teaspoon ground ginger
½ cup toasted chopped walnuts
Garnish: confectioners' sugar

• Preheat oven to 350°. Line an 8-inch square baking pan with parchment paper, letting excess extend over sides of pan on 2 sides. Spray with cooking spray.
• In a small bowl, place raisins and cover with very hot water. Let soak for 1 minute. Drain well.
• In a large bowl, beat together butter, granulated sugar, and brown sugar with a mixer at medium-high speed until light and fluffy, approximately 3 minutes. Beat in egg and then vanilla extract until well combined.
• In a medium bowl, whisk together flour, baking powder, allspice, salt, and ginger. Add to butter mixture, beating until incorporated. Stir in walnuts and drained raisins. Using an offset spatula, spread mixture evenly into prepared pan.
• Bake until edges are golden brown, 20 to 25 minutes. Let cool completely in pan.
• Using parchment overhang as handles, lift from pan and place on cutting surface. Using a sharp knife, cut away browned edges, and then cut into 12 (approximately 2½x1¾-inch) bars. Store in airtight container at room temperature with layers separated with wax paper for up to 3 days.
• Just before serving, garnish with a dusting of confectioners' sugar, if desired.

Chocolate Cake with Peanut Butter Mousse

Makes 1 (8-inch) cake, 12 to 16 servings

2 cups sifted all-purpose flour
2 cups granulated sugar
1 teaspoon baking soda
1 teaspoon salt
½ teaspoon baking powder
¾ cup water
¾ cup whole buttermilk
½ cup unsalted butter, melted and cooled
2 large eggs
4 ounces unsweetened baking chocolate,
   melted and cooled
1 teaspoon vanilla extract
Peanut Butter Mousse (recipe follows)
Garnish: chopped, salted cocktail peanuts

• Preheat oven to 350°. Line 2 (8-inch) square pans with parchment paper. Spray with cooking spray.
• In a large mixing bowl, whisk together flour, sugar, baking soda, salt, and baking powder. Add ¾ cup water, buttermilk, melted butter, eggs, melted chocolate, and vanilla extract, and beat together with mixer at low speed for 30 seconds. Scrape batter down from sides of bowl. Beat at high speed for 3 minutes. (Batter is thin and will splatter, so drape stand mixer with a dish towel or if using a hand mixer, set bowl in a deep sink.) Divide batter between prepared pans, smoothing with an offset spatula. Tap pans on countertop a few times to reduce air bubbles.
• Bake until a wooden pick inserted in centers comes out clean, 27 to 30 minutes. Let cool in pans for 10 minutes, and then turn out onto wire cooling racks, and let cool completely. Wrap cakes in plastic wrap, and let sit at room temperature for 6 to 8 hours.
• Carefully unwrap cake layers. (Cake will be very light and tender.) Place a cake layer, smooth side up, on cake stand. Spread a thick, even layer of Peanut Butter Mousse onto cake. Top with remaining cake layer, smooth side up. Spread a thick layer of remaining mousse on top of cake, using spatula to create swoops in frosting. Spread a layer of mousse onto sides of cake, scraping away some of the mousse for a "naked" look.
• Garnish top of cake with peanuts, if desired. Serve immediately, or keep in a covered container in the refrigerator for up to 3 days. For best texture and flavor, let come to room temperature before serving.

Peanut Butter Mousse

Makes 6 cups

2 (10-ounce) packages peanut butter chips,
   melted and cooled
2 (8-ounce) packages cream cheese, softened
1½ cups creamy peanut butter
1½ cups heavy whipping cream

• In a large bowl, beat together melted chips, cream cheese, and peanut butter with a mixer at medium-high speed until smooth and creamy.
• In a medium bowl, beat heavy cream with a mixer at high speed until soft peaks form. Add to peanut butter mixture, beating at medium-low speed just until combined. Use immediately.

A MILESTONE
Tea Party

The
MENU

SCONE
Strawberries and Cream Scones

🍵 *Gaba Oolong Tea*

SAVORIES
Lobster Salad Tea Sandwiches

Arugula, Lemon, and
Gruyère Quiche

Petite Tomato-Avocado Salads

🍵 *Golden Treasure Black Tea*

SWEETS
French Vanilla Cake with
Coconut-Pecan Frosting

Peach Ice Cream

🍵 *Spiced Masala Chai*
Exotic Indian Blend

Tea Pairings by Grace Tea Company
978-635-9500 • gracetea.com

*Whether turning 30 or 60,
milestone birthdays call
for a regal affair with
decadent tea fare and a
table bedecked with candles
and flowers aplenty.*

- Preheat oven to 350°. Line 2 baking sheets with parchment paper.
- In a medium bowl, whisk together flour, sugar, baking powder, and salt. Using a pastry blender or 2 forks, cut in cold butter until it resembles coarse crumbs. Add freeze-dried strawberries and cream cheese, tossing lightly until coated with flour mixture.
- In a small bowl, combine cold cream and strawberry extract. Add cream mixture to flour mixture, stirring until a dough begins to form. Working gently, bring mixture together with hands until a dough forms. (If dough seems dry, add more cream, 1 tablespoon at a time.)
- Turn out dough onto a lightly floured surface, and knead gently until smooth by patting dough and folding it in half 2 to 3 times. Using a rolling pin, roll out dough to a ½-inch thickness. Using a 2¼-inch round cutter dipped in flour, cut 20 scones from dough, rerolling scraps once. Place scones 2 inches apart on prepared baking sheets.
- Bake until edges of scones are light golden brown, approximately 18 minutes. Let cool on pans for 5 minutes. Remove from pans, and let cool completely on a wire rack.
- Spread Confectioners' Sugar Icing over cooled scones. Serve the same day.

We used freeze-dried berries, such as Just Strawberries, because they contain less water and will not make the scones soggy.

MAKE-AHEAD TIP: *Freeze raw scones on baking sheets. When frozen, transfer scones to resealable plastic bags, and keep frozen until needed. Bake frozen scones as indicated in recipe, allowing an additional 5 to 10 minutes' baking time.*

Confectioners' Sugar Icing
Makes ⅓ cup

1 cup confectioners' sugar
1 tablespoon whole milk

- In a small bowl, whisk together confectioners' sugar and milk until smooth. Use immediately.

Strawberries and Cream Scones
Makes 20

2 cups all-purpose flour
⅓ cup granulated sugar
2 teaspoons baking powder
½ teaspoon salt
4 tablespoons cold salted butter, cubed
½ cup chopped freeze-dried strawberries*
1 (3-ounce) package cream cheese, cubed
¾ cup plus 3 tablespoons cold heavy whipping cream
½ teaspoon strawberry extract
Confectioners' Sugar Icing (recipe follows)

Lobster Salad Tea Sandwiches

Makes 12

4 (3-ounce) lobster tails
3 tablespoons mayonnaise
1 teaspoon fresh lemon juice
½ teaspoon minced fresh tarragon
⅛ teaspoon salt
12 very thin slices white sandwich bread
Garnish: fresh tarragon sprigs

• Place lobster tails in a steamer basket set over a large saucepan containing boiling water. (Do not let water touch steamer basket.) Cover saucepan, and return to a boil. Steam until tails are pink and meat is opaque white, 5 to 7 minutes. Remove tails, and let cool.
• In a medium bowl, whisk together mayonnaise, lemon juice, minced tarragon, and salt.
• Pick lobster meat from tails, and chop very finely. Add lobster to mayonnaise mixture, stirring until combined. Place lobster salad in a covered container, and refrigerate until very cold, approximately 4 hours.
• Spread approximately 2 tablespoons lobster salad each onto 2 bread slices. Stack slices together, lobster sides up, and top with a third slice of bread. Repeat with remaining bread slices and lobster salad to make 4 sandwiches.
• Using a sharp, serrated knife, cut crusts from

sandwiches. Cut each into 3 rectangular sandwiches.
• Garnish with tarragon sprigs, if desired.

MAKE-AHEAD TIP: Sandwiches can be covered with damp paper towels, placed in an airtight container, and refrigerated for up to 4 hours before cutting and serving.

Arugula, Lemon, and Gruyère Quiche

Makes 8 servings

½ (14.1-ounce) package refrigerated piecrust dough
   (1 sheet)
4 cups fresh arugula
1½ cups heavy whipping cream
3 large eggs
1 tablespoon fresh lemon zest
½ teaspoon salt
¼ teaspoon ground black pepper
¼ teaspoon ground nutmeg
2 cups coarsely shredded Gruyère cheese

• Preheat oven to 450°.
• Using a rolling pin and on a lightly floured surface, roll dough into a 12-inch circle. Transfer to a 9-inch removable-bottom tart pan, and referring to page 133, press into bottom and up sides. Trim excess dough. Refrigerate for 30 minutes.

- Prick bottom of dough all over with a fork.
- Bake for 5 minutes. Let cool completely. Reduce oven temperature to 350°.
- Place arugula in a colander, and rinse with water.
- Heat a large nonstick sauté pan over high heat. Add wet arugula; cook, stirring and tossing, just until wilted and tender, approximately 1 minute. Place arugula in a bowl to let cool. Squeeze out excess liquid, and chop finely.
- In a medium bowl, whisk together cream, eggs, lemon zest, salt, pepper, and nutmeg.
- Sprinkle cheese into prepared tart shell. Arrange arugula over cheese. Pour egg mixture over arugula.
- Bake until quiche is slightly puffed and lightly browned, 38 to 40 minutes. Let cool for 15 minutes before cutting and serving.

Petite Tomato-Avocado Salads
Makes 16

2 tablespoons minced fresh basil
1 tablespoon minced fresh chives
1 tablespoon minced fresh parsley
1 tablespoon white wine vinegar
1 teaspoon fresh lemon juice
1 teaspoon fresh lime juice
¼ teaspoon salt
2 tablespoons extra-light olive oil
1 Hass avocado, peeled and pitted
16 cherry tomatoes
Garnish: frisée and minced fresh chives

- In a small bowl, whisk together basil, chives, parsley, vinegar, lemon juice, lime juice, and salt. Add oil in a slow, steady stream, whisking until vinaigrette emulsifies.
- In the work bowl of a food processor, process together avocado and vinaigrette until smooth and creamy. Transfer mixture to a piping bag fitted with a small open star tip (Wilton #21), and refrigerate until ready to use. (Use avocado mixture the same day.)
- Using a small, sharp, serrated knife, partially cut cherry tomatoes vertically into quarters. Cut base of each quarter again with a small cut angled inward. (Each tomato should resemble a flower.) Place on paper towels to absorb moisture.
- Pipe a small amount of avocado purée into center of each cherry tomato.
- Garnish with frisée and chives, if desired. Serve immediately.

French Vanilla Cake with Coconut-Pecan Frosting

Makes 1 (8-inch) cake, approximately 12 servings

½ cup salted butter, softened
1 cup granulated sugar
2 large eggs
1 tablespoon vanilla extract
2 cups cake flour
2 teaspoons baking powder
¼ teaspoon salt
½ cup whole milk
Coconut-Pecan Frosting (recipe follows)

• Preheat oven to 350°. Spray 2 (8-inch) round cake pans with baking spray with flour.
• In a large bowl, beat together butter and sugar with a mixer at medium speed until fluffy, 3 to 4 minutes, stopping to scrape sides of bowl. Add eggs, one at a time, beating well after each addition. Beat in vanilla extract.

• In a medium bowl, whisk together flour, baking powder, and salt. With mixer at low speed, gradually add flour mixture to butter mixture alternately with milk, beginning and ending with flour mixture, beating just until combined after each addition. Divide batter between prepared pans.
• Bake until cake layers are golden brown and a wooden pick inserted in centers comes out clean, approximately 25 minutes. Let cool in pans for 10 minutes. Remove from pans, and let cool completely on wire racks.
• Using a long serrated knife, cut each cake layer horizontally into 2 layers. Spread Coconut-Pecan Frosting between layers and on top of cake. Cover and store at room temperature, or refrigerate for up to 3 days, if desired.

MAKE-AHEAD TIP: Cake layers can be made up to 1 week in advance, wrapped tightly in plastic wrap, and frozen until needed. Let thaw in refrigerator before spreading with frosting.

Coconut-Pecan Frosting

Makes 2½ cups

1 cup pecan halves
1 cup granulated sugar
1 cup heavy whipping cream
3 large egg yolks, lightly beaten
½ cup salted butter, cubed
⅛ teaspoon salt
1½ cups sweetened flaked coconut
¾ teaspoon vanilla extract

• Preheat oven to 350°.
• Place pecans on a rimmed baking sheet. Bake until very lightly browned, approximately 5 minutes. Let cool completely before finely chopping.
• In a medium saucepan, stir together sugar, cream, egg yolks, butter, and salt. Cook over medium heat, stirring constantly, until mixture comes to a boil. Immediately remove from heat.
• Add pecans, coconut, and vanilla extract, stirring to combine. Let cool until a spreadable consistency is reached, approximately 30 minutes.

Peach Ice Cream

Makes 1 quart

2 cups heavy whipping cream
1 cup whole milk
3 large egg yolks
¾ cup granulated sugar
¼ teaspoon salt
2 teaspoons vanilla extract
1¾ cups chopped peeled fresh peaches
Garnish: fresh mint

• In a medium saucepan, heat together cream and milk over medium heat, stirring frequently, just until bubbles form around edges of pan. (Do not boil.)
• In a medium bowl, whisk together egg yolks, sugar, and salt until light and creamy. Add ¼ cup hot cream mixture to egg mixture, whisking vigorously. Add ½ cup hot cream mixture to egg mixture, whisking vigorously. Slowly add remaining hot cream mixture, whisking constantly. Return mixture to saucepan, and cook over medium heat, stirring with a wooden spoon, until mixture coats back of spoon, approximately 5 minutes. (Do not boil.)

• Remove from heat, and pour through a fine-mesh strainer into a metal or heatproof glass bowl. Add vanilla extract, stirring to combine. Set bowl into a larger bowl of ice, and let cool completely, stirring frequently. Transfer custard to a covered container, and refrigerate overnight.
• In the work bowl of a food processor, purée peaches until smooth. (You should have approximately 1¼ cups.) Add peach purée to cold custard. Pour mixture into a 1½-quart countertop ice cream maker. Freeze according to manufacturer's instructions. Transfer ice cream to an airtight container, and freeze until ready to serve.
• Garnish individual servings with mint, if desired.

How-tos

Let these step-by-step photos serve as your visual guide
while you create these impressive and delicious teatime treats.

TARTLET CRUST

Herbed Asparagus Quiches **34** | Chocolate-Mascarpone Tartlets **48**
Mini Tartlet Shells **48** | Raspberry Tartlets **60** | Tartlet Shells **60**
Apple-Blackberry Tartlets **119** | Arugula, Lemon, and Gruyère Quiche **129**

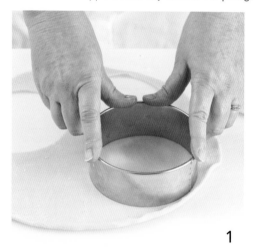

1

Using a cutter, cut shapes from dough.

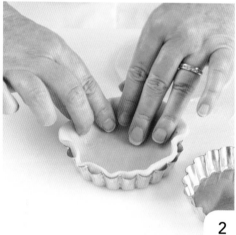

2

Press dough shapes into tartlet pans.

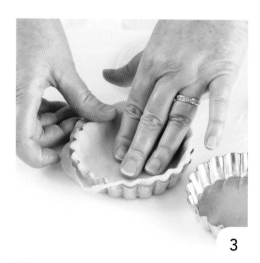

3

Trim excess dough.

4

Using the wide end of a chopstick, push dough
into indentations of pan.

Acknowledgments

EDITOR Lorna Reeves
ART DIRECTOR Leighann Lott Bryant
ASSOCIATE EDITOR Britt E. Stafford
SENIOR COPY EDITOR Rhonda Lee Lother
EDITORIAL ASSISTANT Katherine Cloninger
SENIOR DIGITAL IMAGING SPECIALIST
Delisa McDaniel
DIGITAL IMAGING SPECIALIST
Clark Densmore

COVER
Photography by William Dickey
Food Styling by Kathleen Kanen • Recipe Development by Janet Lambert • Styling by Courtni Bodiford
Shelley Rose, Pansy, Forget Me Not teapot, flat cup and saucer set, and sugar bowl from Replacements, Ltd., 800-737-5223, *replacements.com*. Rosanna *Les Desserts* round skirted pedestal from Rosanna Inc., 877-343-3779, *rosannainc.com*. Heritage Lace *Victorian Rose* tablecloth from Heritage Lace, 641-628-4949, *heritagelace.com*.

A STYLISH CELEBRATION
Photography by William Dickey
Food Styling by Kathleen Kanen • Recipe Development by Taylor Franklin Wann and Laura Crandall
Styling by Courtni Bodiford
Pages 15–26: Deshoulières *Vignes White* teapot, teacup, dessert plate, sugar bowl, and oval platter; *Vignes Blue* dinner plate, saucer, creamer, rectangular cake plate, and round cake platter from BIA Cordon Bleu, 800-242-2210, *biacordonbleu.bridgecatalog.com*. Cambridge Silversmiths *Conversation Gold Satin* 5-piece place setting from Cambridge Silversmiths, 973-227-4400, *cambridgesilversmiths.com*. Hemstich place mat and *Gold Flower* metal taper candle holder from Pier 1, 817-252-6300, *pier1.com*. Buffet napkins, glass tube 3-tier vase, gold modern bell taper candleholder, and square white *Capiz* tealight candleholders from World Market, 877-967-5362, *worldmarket.com*. Blue vases and candleholders from Hobby Lobby, 855-329-7060, *hobbylobby.com*. Location courtesy of Anna Blair Gribbin.

PARISIAN SOIRÉE
Photography by Jim Bathie
Recipe Development/Food Styling by Janet Lambert
Styling by Courtni Bodiford
Pages 27–38: Royal Albert *Dimity Rose* teapot, footed cup and saucer set, salad plate; Royal Stafford *Berkeley Rose* teapot, mini creamer, and sugar bowl; Philippe Deshoulières *Orsay White* dinner plates; Gorham Silver *Melrose* modern hollow knife, salad fork, teaspoon, and sugar tongs from Replacements, Ltd., 800-737-5223, *replacements.com*. Pink-and-white cup and saucer sets for party favors from Paris In A Cup, 714-538-9411, *parisinacup.com*. (Macarons, gift bags, and gift tags not included.) Napkins and napkin rings from Pier 1, 817-252-6300, *pier1.com*. Eiffel Tower metal wall decor from Hobby Lobby, 855-329-7060, *hobbylobby.com*. Small Eiffel towers, gold vase centerpiece, and assorted bedazzled stands from HomeGoods, 800-888-0776, *homegoods.com*. Jewel-studded cake stand with dome from TJ Maxx, 833-888-0776, *tjmaxx.tjx.com*. Floral arrangements by Lindsey Harrington at Furbished Nest, 205-913-4841, *thefurbishednest@gmail.com*. Location courtesy of Carole Brightbill.

TEATIME SURPRISE
Photography by John O'Hagan
Recipe Development/Food Styling by Janet Lambert
Styling by Lucy Wilson
Pages 39–50: Herend *Printemps* teapot, salad plate, teacup, saucer, creamer, rectangular tray, oval platter, and covered sugar with rose; *Printemps Blue Border* dinner plate from Herend, 800-643-7363, *herendusa .com*. Rosanna small white pedestal from Rosanna Inc., 877-343-3779, *rosannainc.com*. Sferra *Festival* napkins and place mats in *Ocean* from Sferra, 877-336-2003, *sferra.com*. Flower arrangements from FlowerBuds, 205-970-3223, *flowerbudsfloristbirmingham.com*. Location courtesy of Sondra Massengale.

BUTTERFLY-KISSED BIRTHDAY
Photography by Marcy Black Simpson
Recipe Development/Food Styling by Janet Lambert
Styling by Lucy Wilson
Pages 51–62: Grace's Teaware *Blue Butterfly* teapot, footed cup and saucer set, and square salad plate; *Pink Butterfly* creamer, sugar bowl, and lid from Replacements, Ltd., 800-737-5223, *replacements.com*. Wallace *Queens* 65-piece flatware set from Mikasa, 866-645-2721, *mikasa.com*. Butterfly cupcake wrappers and butterflies blue and lavender hues wafer paper from Fancy Flours, 406-587-0118, *fancyflours .com*. Pink linen and flower vases from Pottery Barn, 888-779-5176, *potterybarn.com*. Round paper doilies from Sur La Table, 800-243-0852, *surlatable.com*.

A GRAND OCCASION
Photography by Jim Bathie
Recipe Development/Food Styling by Janet Lambert
Styling by Courtni Bodiford
Pages 63–74: Rosenthal-Continental *Diplomat* teapot, flat cup and saucer set, sugar bowl with lid, dinner plate, salad plate, creamer, square vegetable bowl, and handled cake plate; Castleton (USA) *Sunnyvale* round vegetable bowl (for centerpiece) and 13-inch oval serving platter; Wallace Silver *Rose Point* demitasse spoon, new French hollow knife, salad fork, and teaspoon from Replacements, Ltd., 800-737-5223, *replacements .com*. Anna Weatherley *Anna's Palette* chargers in Meadow Green from Devine Corp, 732-751-0500, *devinecorp.net*. Hemstich napkin and beaded napkin ring from Pier 1, 817-252-6300, *pier1.com*. Floral arrangement by Lindsey Harrington at Furbished Nest, 205-913-4841, *thefurbishednest@gmail.com*.

A FAIRY-TALE BIRTHDAY
Photography by John O'Hagan
Recipe Development/Food Styling by Virginia Hornbuckle
Styling by Courtni Bodiford
Pages 75–88: Anna Weatherley *Budapest Spring* flat cup and saucer set, *Simply Anna Polka* salad plate and charger, *Waterlily Seascape* flat cup and saucer set, *Garden Party* 10-inch round pierced bowl, and *Ivy Garland* 17-inch oval serving platter; Godinger *Jardin* teapot, creamer, sugar bowl with lid, canapé plate, and square bowl; Towle Silver *Old Master* five o'clock spoon, salad fork, hollow handle knife, and cake server from Replacements, Ltd., 800-737-5223, *replacements.com*. Woodland villages, green runner, and fairy figures from Michaels, 800-642-4235, *michaels.com*. Butterfly wings on benches and fairy wands from Amazon, 888-280-4331, *amazon.com*. Location courtesy of Shoppe BHM, 205-224-4450, *shoppebhm.com*.

SWEET CELEBRATION
Photography by Jim Bathie
Recipe Development/Food Styling by Janet Lambert
Styling by Courtni Bodiford
Pages 89–98: Shelley Rose, Pansy, Forget Me Not teapot, flat cup and saucer set, salad plate, creamer, sugar bowl with lid, and oval vegetable bowl; Royal Winton *Old Cottage Chintz* dinner plate and rectangular serving platter; Oneida Silver *Cantata* salad fork, modern knife, teaspoon, and demitasse spoon from Replacements, Ltd., 800-737-5223, *replacements .com*. Cake stand from HomeGoods, 800-888-0776, *homegoods.com*. Heritage Lace Victorian Rose tablecloth from Heritage Lace, 641-628-4949, *heritagelace.com*. Sandwich tray and hemstitch napkin from Pier 1, 817-252-6300, *pier1.com*. Floral arrangements by and location courtesy of Bronwyn Cardwell.

TEA-REX BIRTHDAY
Photography by William Dickey
Recipe Development/Food Styling by Virginia Hornbuckle
Styling by Courtni Bodiford
Pages 99–110: Calamityware *Things Could Be Worse* teapot, sugar, creamer, and mugs; *Now What* small plates; *Dinosaurs* platter; and *Pterodactyl* plate from Calamityware, *calamityware.com*. Montes Doggett *Two Hundred Eighty Eight* cake stand from Bromberg's, 205-871-3276, *brombergs.com*. Two-tier stand from Target, 800-591-3869, *target.com*. Calvin Klein *Yuzen* tablecloth from Amazon, 888-280-4331, *amazon.com*. Succulents and planters from Home Depot, 800-466-3337, *homedepot.com*. Blue, green, orange, and red dinosaurs from Hobby Lobby, 855-329-7060, *hobbylobby.com*. *Mateo* navy napkin and napkin ring from Pier 1, 817-252-6300, *pier1.com*. Location courtesy of Anna McClendon.

GENTLEMANLY BIRTHDAY
Photography by John O'Hagan
Recipe Development/Food Styling by Janet Lambert
Styling by Courtni Bodiford
Pages 111–122: Spode *Woodland* teapot and lid, flat cup and saucer set, hexagonal bowl (for flowers), dinner plates, salad plates, sugar bowl with lid, creamer, bread tray, rectangular serving platter, and large sandwich tray; Wilton Armetale *Bishop White* Old French knife, salad fork, and teaspoon from Replacements, Ltd., 800-737-5223, *replacements.com*. Napkins from World Market, 877-967-5362, *worldmarket.com*. Vagabond House wood flatware caddy with elk head handles, Match Pewter oval tray, and Carmel Ceramica condiment dishes from Bromberg's, 205-871-3276, *brombergs.com*. Rosanna *Décor Bon Bon* square pedestal from Rosanna Inc., 877-343-3779, *rosannainc.com*. Floral arrangement by Lindsey Harrington at Furbished Nest, 205-913-4841, *thefurbishednest@ gmail.com*. Location courtesy of Mallory Smith.

A MILESTONE TEA PARTY
Photography by Marcy Black Simpson
Recipe Development/Food Styling by Janet Lambert
Styling by Lucy Wilson
Pages 123–132: Royal Worcester *Regency Blue* 5-piece place setting, teapot, and oval platter; Candlewick platter from Replacements, 800-737-5223, *replacements.com*. Hemstitched linens from Bromberg's, 205-871-3276, *brombergs.com*. Floral arrangements by FlowerBuds, 205-970-3223, *flowerbudsfloristbirmingham.com*.

Recipe Index

EDITOR'S NOTE: Recipe titles shown in gold are gluten-free, provided gluten-free versions of processed ingredients (such as flours and extracts) are used.